Miroslaw Balka
How It Is

556371

D0541832

Tate, Friends, Family
Thank You
MB

Miroslaw Balka
How It Is

Edited by
Helen Sainsbury

Contributions by
Zygmunt Bauman
Paulo Herkenhoff
Julian Heynen
László Krasznahorkai

Tate Publishing

The Unilever Series:
an annual art commision sponsored by Unilever

Unilever

First published 2009 by order of the Tate Trustees
by Tate Publishing, a division of Tate Enterprises
Ltd, Millbank, London SW1P 4RG
www.tate.org.uk/publishing
on the occasion of the exhibition at
Tate Modern, London
13 October 2009 – 5 April 2010

A catalogue record for this book is available from
the British Library

ISBN 978 1 85437 847 7

Distributed in the United States and Canada
by Harry N. Abrams, Inc., New York

Library of Congress Control Number: 2009928895

Designed by APFEL (A Practice for Everyday Life)
Printed by PUSH, United Kingdom
Front cover by APFEL (inspired by Roy Kuhlman's
design for the front cover of Samuel Beckett's *How
It Is,* Grove Press, New York 1964)

FSC
Mixed Sources
Product group from well-managed
forests and other controlled sources
Cert no. SGS-COC-004556
www.fsc.org
© 1996 Forest Stewardship Council

Contents

Sponsor's Foreword

Miroslaw Balka's *How It Is* marks the tenth commission in The Unilever Series. Like the nine artists who preceded him, Balka has found an intriguing and thought-provoking way to fill the space in Tate Modern's vast Turbine Hall.

Unilever is very proud of its long-term partnership with Tate Modern. Indeed, the annual unveiling of The Unilever Series commission has become a key date in the diary for anyone who has an interest in modern art. From Olafur Eliasson's *The Weather Project* to Rachel Whiteread's *EMBANKMENT*, the series has facilitated some of the most memorable contemporary art of the past decade.

Even more gratifying is the fact that, since the partnership began, more than twenty-two million people have passed through Tate Modern's doors to view one of the installations.

Unilever's association with Tate Modern also extends to the sponsorship of an international online education programme called *The Unilever Series: turbine-generation*. Now in its second year, the scheme enables children from around the world to explore and share their thoughts on a range of cultural issues through a variety of different art forms.

We hope that you enjoy and are inspired by Miroslaw Balka's work.

Paul Polman
Group Chief Executive, Unilever plc

Director's Foreword

The Turbine Hall at Tate Modern is now synonymous with the Unilever commission, as for the past nine years it has been annually transformed by some of the most important artists working today. The hall is unique in both its architecture and function; it is simultaneously public piazza and gallery, and both artists and visitors respond to the space in surprising and unpredictable ways. This year, it is a great honour to stage the tenth commission in The Unilever Series, a uniquely ambitious work by Miroslaw Balka: *How It Is.*

Balka is one of the most significant contemporary artists of his generation, whose work has won international critical acclaim. Balka's works explore themes of personal experience, often set within the context of the history of his native country, Poland. His work may appear minimal in its aesthetic – pared down forms are created from simple materials ranging from concrete and steel to soap, ash and human hair – yet these choices are steeped in both personal and, most crucially, universal meanings.

How It Is embodies these concerns, whilst also responding to the architecture of the space and focusing specifically on the viewer's encounter. In conceiving this work Balka has drawn upon innumerable personal, collective, historical and fictional references, which are discussed in

detail by the authors in this catalogue. However the presence and experience of the audience is key. Upon entering the dark interior of the sculpture viewers will complete the work; yet rather than creating a stage or spectacle, the container focuses the audience inwards, both physically and psychologically, as they enter into the unknown.

How It Is is testament to Balka's poetic ability to explore seemingly insurmountable themes with great intelligence and insight, and we cannot thank him enough for developing this extraordinary commission. He has worked closely with Helen Sainsbury, Curatorial Programme Manager, who has led the project with dedication and professionalism. Many thanks go to her and to Kathy Noble and Maeve Polkinhorn who have made valuable contributions to the project as Assistant Curators. We are also grateful to Phil Monk, Art Installation Manager; Dennis Ahern, Head of Operations, and Adrian Hardwicke, Director of Visitor Services and Estates whose work with the design team was crucial to realising the project. The design and production of the work has been developed with the expertise and enthusiasm of Shonn Mills of Ramboll UK, and Jason Waddy of Gardiner & Theobald Management Services, working in close collaboration with Neil Fry, Steve Horrod and Bill Tustin at

Littlehampton Welding Ltd. Special thanks are due to Andy Mottershaw and his installation team for bringing such pride and passion to the project. We are also very grateful to Alex Bradley at White Cube for her kind support and, in collaboration with MDM Props, for finding the most appropriate solution for the 'darkness'. We are also extremely grateful for the support of Balka's galleries, in particular Jay Jopling and White Cube, London.

Projects of this complexity necessitate the work of a dedicated team across Tate. We would like to thank the following colleagues and their teams: Julian Bird, Chief Operating Officer; Nicky White, Marina Busse and Emilie Janvrin from Development; Bomi Odufunade from Press; Livia Ratcliffe from Marketing; Simon Bolitho from Interpretation; Jane Burton, Kate Vogel, Kirstie Beaven and Jared Schiller from Tate Media.

We would also like to thank everyone whose efforts went towards the creation of this catalogue, which has been edited by Helen Sainsbury and Miroslaw Balka with the expert guidance of Rebecca Fortey. We are most grateful to Paulo Herkenhoff and Julian Heynen for contributing such illuminating essays covering both the artist's work and his myriad of influences, and to Zygmunt Bauman and László Krasznahorkai whose thought-provoking contributions add another dimension to our understanding of the themes behind Balka's work. Thanks are also due to Fiona Elliott and George Szirtes for their sensitive translations of the texts by Julian Heynen and László Krasznahorkai respectively. Many thanks also to Roger Thorp, Melissa Larner, Deborah Metherell and Emma Woodiwiss for steering the catalogue expertly through the complex editorial and production process. Finally, we would like to extend our special thanks to our designers at APFEL (A Practice for Everyday Life), for their astute understanding of the concept and for creating such an intuitive and elegant design.

We are extremely grateful to Unilever for its continuing sponsorship of The Unilever Series commission, this outstanding series of artists' projects in the Turbine Hall. Its unwavering support is invaluable to Tate Modern and its visitors. We offer Unilever, the CEO Paul Polman and Senior Vice President of Global Communications Gavin Neath, our most sincere thanks. Without this level of support projects of this scale and ambition would simply not be possible.

Vicente Todolí
Director, Tate Modern

On Velocity

László
Krasznahorkai

Translated by
George Szirtes

I want to leave Earth behind, so I dash past the bridge over the stream by the meadow, past the reindeer-feeder in the dark of the forest, turning at Monowitz on the corner of Schuhkammer and Kleiderkammer, into the street in my desire to move faster than the Earth in whatever direction this thought has taken from the point it started, for everything has converged to such a point of departure, leaving everything behind, leaving behind the Earth, and I set off, rushing instinctively, doing the right thing by rushing because it wasn't East or South or North I was heading or in some other direction in relation to these, but West, which was right, if only because the Earth spins from left to right, that is to say from a western to an eastern direction, because that is right, that's how things are, that's how it felt right, was right, from the first half-fraction of the instant in which I started, since everything moves most definitely from West to East, the building, the morning kitchen, the table with its cup, the cup with its steaming emerald-coloured tea and the way the scent spirals upward and all the blades of grass in the meadow that are pearled with morning dew, and the empty reindeer-feeder in the dark of the forest, all of these, each and every one, moves according to its nature from West to East, that's to say towards me, I who wanted to move faster than Earth, and rushed through the door over the meadow and the dark of the forest, and had to move precisely in a western direction while everything else, the whole of creation, the lot, each billionth of a billionth component of this overwhelmingly vast world, was continuously spinning at unimaginable speed from West to East; or rather I, who wanted to move faster, therefore fixed my own speed in the opposite, wholly unexpected, direction, one beyond the realm of physics, that's to say having chosen to do so with self-evidently instinctive freedom, had therefore to run counter to it, counter to this terrifying world and everything in it that comprises corner, meadow and forest, or rather, no, as I painfully realised in the second half of the instant, no alas, of course not in that direction, opposing its movement being precisely the worst choice, my instincts had led me to turn in precisely the wrong direction at the corner, over the field and past the dark of the forest, when I should have chosen to move in the same direction, from West to East as Earth did in its, O! Entirety, and so, in the blinking of an eye, I immediately turned about my axis wondering how my instincts could have led me to move so firmly in the direction opposite the Earth's movement since, if I did what I was doing now, its speed would be the same as mine, its and mine the same, they would have a positive relation to each other, combining with each other to greater effect, would, in effect, be doing the same thing, the Earth turning from West to East, I moving from West to East, the majestic immovability of the starting point being assumed to be an absolute value, so that it would be practically impossible to see how the smaller part belonged to the Greater Whole, and how the Greater Movement would allow space for the little counter-movement, the one independent of the other, the two linked only in one way, in that the Greater Movement permitted the small counter-direction to function within it, and what a short-circuit that would be, I concluded as I was already turning, but then why was I thinking this, instinctively thinking moreover, since if I were talking about one single relationship, then that single relationship could be no other than that of one term comprehending the other, so that one contained the other, so that one was part of the other, its subservient part, its subsidiary, its little brother, its little sister, carried by the Greater whichever way it moved, and that Earth was quite certainly, and indeed correctly, moving in the one direction it could move, that is from West to East, and I was a part of it, inside it, I who had desired to be faster than the Earth to whose movement mine was demonstrably related, in, moreover, the most strictly logical way, since the velocity, that is to say of the Earth, contained my velocity, my sprinting, the fact being, one way or the other, that whatever else Earth did, its velocity certainly comprised mine, after all whatever Grand Perspective was employed it didn't matter whether I ran counter to its direction of movement, that is to say registering as a minus quantity, or in the same direction as it, that is constituting a plus, it was just that, to me personally, it was a matter of supreme importance since it was this precisely I wanted, that is, to move faster than the Earth, in other words it was the plus, the positive value, I needed, that's to say what mattered was to have the Little Independent Micrototality moving within the Great Free Macrototality as part of it, but the fact is I was simply running within the Great Inwardness of the Laws of Physics, but this time in absolutely the right direction, that is to say from West to East, according with the movement of the Earth, since it is precisely in this fashion, in precisely this manner, of course, I'd have to run in order to be faster than the Earth, running with it so to speak, from West to East, from a western direction to an eastern direction, and − suddenly the thought hit me like a bolt of lightning − that I was already faster, since my velocity now comprehended that of the Earth, that is to say it comprehended it without me having to do much more than move a muscle, and that this way, by running over Earth's surface from West to East, I had made the task so much simpler, that I could breathe ever more easily, since it was fresh out here, enjoying the night of freedom or the dawn of freedom, or something between the two, and that I was locked into that interval between night and dawn, feeling perfectly calm, because the thought of having now chosen the correct direction meant I was moving faster than the Earth, since Earth is thought, as I thought, right at the beginning, and now I wanted to move faster than thought, to leave thought behind, and that that had suddenly become my aim, so it was what I did when I turned at Monowitz on the corner of Schuhkammer and Kleiderkammer, across the meadow with its pearly grass, past the bridge over the stream, beyond the dark of the forest, passing the empty reindeer-feeder, so it was right that I should have set out in the wrong direction at first, on instinct, and then corrected myself and quick as blinking turned and moved in the right direction, from West to East, a small micrototality within the Greater Macrototality, in which case I had only to add my speed to its speed, which I did, running as fast as I could, my feet pounding on under the enormous sky that was changing from night to dawn, and there was nothing in my head but the sense that everything was as it should be, that I was simply contributing my share of velocity to the Earth's, my velocity to its velocity, when suddenly a new thought struck me that, fine, this was all very well, but how did my speed relate to that of the Earth, how much faster was I, and was that an interesting question in the first place? That is to say the question of how much faster I was than the Earth. And no, it's not interesting, I said to myself, my feet pounding all the while as normal, since all that was interesting was that I should move faster than thought, that is to say, outrun the Earth, but then the little brother within me started making calculations in my head, arguing that there, on the one hand, was the Earth's velocity, that majestically challenging, vast, eternal per secundum and there, on the other, were my best efforts at running at whatever per secundum the occasion offered, and then, it seemed to me, any relative value would do for me to run ahead of the Earth, that I needn't run particularly fast since it would make very little difference to my overall relative speed if I did slow down a bit, so I immediately slowed, and it was clear as clear could be that there were innumerable ways of being faster than Earth, it being enough for me to continue in a West to East direction, and enough simply to run because putting aside the magnetic drag of the various latitudes which would cumulatively increase, there being an infinite number of velocities to choose from, infinite values were therefore available for my own running-speed and what is more, I thought, further decreasing my velocity all the while, the fact is it would be enough if ... if I moved at all, just put one foot in front of the other, the essential thing being to move in a West to East direction, enough simply not to stay still, since there were billions on billions of possible velocities in which case I was free, entirely free, or so I observed as my steps instinctively slowed, perfectly free to choose just how fast I moved since any movement in the right direction would result in moving faster than the Earth and therefore faster than thought, since Earth is itself thought, and that was the way I was thinking, even before I started the whole process a little while ago, the way I was thinking when I dashed past the bridge over the stream by the meadow, past the reindeer-feeder in the dark of the forest and turned at Monowitz on the corner of Schuhkammer and Kleiderkammer. Providing I make no mistakes, I told myself, providing I keep going in the right direction, providing I simply move, just carry on walking through the fresh dawn air, I would achieve what I had set out to do, and be faster than the Earth – it was just the darkness of the forest that would recede into the distance, just the meadow, the corner, just the scent of that emerald-coloured mist vanishing into time for ever, into infinity, beyond recall.

Strangers Are Dangers ... Are They?

Zygmunt
Bauman

Whatever happens to cities in the course of their history, one feature remains constant: they are spaces where strangers move in close proximity to each other. The ubiquitous presence of strangers, constantly within sight and reach, inserts a large dose of perpetual uncertainty into all city-dwellers' life pursuits; that presence is a prolific and never-resting source of anxiety and of a usually dormant, yet constantly erupting, aggressiveness.

Strangers provide a convenient outlet for our inborn fear of the unknown, uncertain and unpredictable. In chasing strangers away from our homes and streets, the frightening ghost of uncertainty is, even if only for a moment, exorcised: the horrifying monster of insecurity is burnt in effigy. Despite those exorcisms, however, our 'liquid-modern' life remains stubbornly uncertain, erratic and capricious.[1]

The stranger is, by definition, an agent moved by intentions of which we can at best guess, but of which we can never be sure. In all the equations we compose when deliberating on what to do and how to behave, the stranger is an unknown variable. The stranger is, after all, 'strange': a bizarre being, whose intentions and reactions may be thoroughly different from those of the ordinary (familiar) folks. And so, even when not behaving aggressively or explicitly resented, strangers are discomforting: their sheer presence makes a tall order of the already daunting task of predicting the effects of action and its chances of success. And yet the sharing of space with strangers, living (as a rule uninvited and unwelcome) in proximity to strangers, is a condition that city residents find difficult, perhaps impossible, to escape.

Since the proximity of strangers is the urban dwellers' non-negotiable fate, some *modus vivendi* able to make cohabitation palatable and life liveable must be designed, tried and tested. The way in which we go about gratifying this need is, however, a matter of *choice*. And we make these choices daily – whether by commission or omission, by design or default; whether consciously or just by following, blindly and mechanically, customary patterns; whether through wide-ranging discussion and deliberation, or just through following the trusted or currently fashionable means. Opting out of the search for a *modus vivendi* is another of the possible choices.

Of São Paulo, for instance – the largest, bustling and fast expanding

Brazilian city – Teresa Caldeira writes: 'São Paulo is today a city of walls. Physical barriers have been constructed everywhere – around houses, apartment buildings, parks, squares, office complexes and schools … A new aesthetics of security shapes all types of constructions and imposes a new logic of surveillance and distance.'[2] Those who can afford it, buy themselves into a 'condominium', in its intention essentially a hermitage: physically inside, but socially and spiritually outside the city. 'Closed communities are supposed to be separate worlds. Their advertisements propose a total "way of life" which would represent an alternative to the quality of life offered by the city and its deteriorated public space.'

The most prominent feature of the condominium is its 'isolation and distance from the city … Isolation means separation from those considered to be socially inferior' and, as the developers and the real-estate agents insist, 'the key factor to assure this is security. This means fences and walls surrounding the condominium, guards on duty twenty-four hours a day controlling the entrances, and an array of facilities and services for keeping the others out.'

As we all know, fences cannot but have two sides. Fences divide the otherwise continuous space into an 'inside' and an 'outside', but what is the 'inside' for those on one side of the fence is the 'outside' for those on the other. The residents of

The Paraisópolis favela, which borders the affluent district of Morumbi in São Paulo, Brazil, 2005

condominiums fence themselves out of the hurly-burly life of the city in an oasis of calm and safety. By the same token, though, they fence all the others out of the decent and agreeable, secure places, and into their own shabby and squalid streets. The fence separates the 'voluntary ghetto' of the high and mighty from the enforced ghettos of the low and hapless. For the insiders of the voluntary ghetto, the other ghettoes are 'we won't go in' spaces. For the insiders of the involuntary ones, the area to which they have been confined is the 'we can't get out' space.

Paradoxically, originally constructed to provide safety for all their inhabitants, cities are these days associated more often with danger than with security.

As Nan Elin puts it the 'fear factor has certainly grown, as indicated by the growth in locked car and house doors and security systems, the popularity of "gated" and "secure" communities for all age and income groups, and the increasing surveillance of public spaces, not to mention the unending reports of danger emitted by the mass media'.[3]

Genuine and putative threats to the body and the property of the individual are turning fast into major considerations whenever the merits or disadvantages of a living place are assessed. Threats have also been assigned the topmost position in real-estate marketing policy. Uncertainty regarding the future, the frailty of social position and existential insecurity, those ubiquitous

Housing development in Phoenix, Arizona, 2009

accompaniments of life in the liquid-modern world, are rooted notoriously in remote places, yet the passions they generate tend to be focused on the nearest targets, and channelled into concerns with personal safety; the kind of concerns that condense in turn into segregationist/exclusionist urges, inexorably leading to urban space wars.

As we can learn from the perceptive study by American architectural/urban critic, Steven Flusty,[4] servicing those wars and, particularly, designing the ways by which to deny adversaries access to the claimed space, are the most salient concerns of architectural innovation and urban development in American cities. The most proudly advertised novelties are 'interdictory spaces' – 'designed to intercept, repel or filter the would-be users'. Explicitly, the purpose of 'interdictory spaces' is to divide, segregate and exclude – not to build bridges, easy passages and hospitable meeting places; not to facilitate, but to break communication, and to separate, rather than bring people together. The architectural/urbanistic inventions listed and named by Flusty are the technically updated equivalents of pre-modern moats, turrets and embrasures of the city walls, only instead of defending the city and all its inhabitants against the enemy outside, they are built to set the city's residents apart. Among the inventions named by Flusty, there is 'slippery space' – 'space that cannot be reached, due to contorted, protracted, or missing paths of approach'; 'prickly space' – 'space that cannot be

comfortably occupied, defended by such details as wall-mounted sprinkler heads activated to clear loiterers, or ledges sloped to inhibit sitting'; and 'jittery space' – 'space that cannot be utilised unobserved due to active monitoring by roving patrols and/or remote technologies feeding to security stations'. All these and others like them have but one purpose: to cut off extraterritorial enclaves, to erect little fortresses inside which the members of the supra-territorial global elite may groom, cultivate and relish their bodily independence and spiritual isolation from locality. These developments described by Flusty are high-tech manifestations of the ubiquitous 'mixophobia', a widespread reaction to the mind-boggling, spine-chilling and nerve-racking variegation of human types and lifestyles that rub shoulders in the streets of contemporary cities and in 'ordinary' (read: unprotected by 'interdictory spaces') living districts. Giving vent to segregationist urges may relieve the rising tension. Confusing and disconcerting differences might be unassailable and intractable, but perhaps the toxin may be squeezed out of their sting by assigning to each form of life its separate, isolated, well-marked and well-guarded physical space. Perhaps one could secure for oneself, for one's kith and kin and other 'people like oneself', a territory free from that jumble and mess that irredeemably poisons other city areas.

'Mixophobia' manifests itself in a drive towards islands of similarity and sameness amidst the sea of variety and difference. The reasons for mixophobia are banal – easy to understand, if not necessarily easy to forgive. As Richard Sennett suggests,[5] 'the "we" feeling, which expresses a desire to be similar, is a way for men to avoid the necessity of looking deeper into each other'. It promises thereby some spiritual comfort: the prospect of facilitating togetherness by making redundant the efforts to understand, negotiate and compromise. 'Innate to the process of forming a coherent image of community is the desire to avoid actual participation. Feeling common bonds without common experience occurs in the first place because men are afraid of participation, afraid of the dangers and the challenges of it, afraid of its pain.' The drive towards a 'community of similarity' is a sign of withdrawal not just from the otherness outside, but also from the commitment to the lively yet turbulent, engaged yet cumbersome interaction inside.

Choosing the escape option prompted by mixophobia has an insidious and deleterious consequence of its own: the more self-perpetuating and self-reinforcing the strategy, the more it is ineffective. The more time people spend in the company of others 'like them' – with whom they 'socialise' perfunctorily and matter-of-factly without risk of miscomprehension, and without the onerous need to translate between distinct universes of meaning – the more they are likely to 'de-learn' the art of negotiating shared meanings and a mutual *modus vivendi*. As they fail to learn or forget the skills needed to live with difference, or neglect to acquire them, they view the prospect

of confronting strangers face-to-face with rising apprehension. Strangers tend to appear ever more frightening as they become increasingly alien, unfamiliar and incomprehensible, and as the mutual communication that could eventually assimilate their 'otherness' to one's own life-world fades, or never takes off in the first place. The drive to a homogeneous, territorially isolated environment may be triggered by mixophobia; but practising territorial separation is mixophobia's life-blood.

Mixophobia, though, is not the sole combatant on the urban battlefield. City living is a notoriously ambivalent experience. It attracts *and* repels, and it is the same aspects of city life that, intermittently or simultaneously, attract and repel. The variety of the urban environment is a source of fear, yet the same twinkling urban scenery, never short of novelty and surprise, exerts an irresistible charm and seductive power.

The never-ending and constantly dazzling spectacle of the city is not therefore experienced unambiguously as a curse; nor does sheltering from it feel like an un-mixed blessing. The city prompts mixophilia as much as mixophobia. City life is an intrinsically and irreparably ambivalent affair. The bigger and more heterogeneous a city, the more attractions it may support and offer. The massive concentration of strangers is, simultaneously, a repellent and a powerful magnet, drawing to the city ever new cohorts of men and women weary of the monotony of rural or small-town life, fed up with its repetitive routine – and despairing of the dearth of chances. Variety is a promise of opportunities, many and different, fitting all skills and tastes. It seems that mixophilia, just like mixophobia, is a self-propelling, self-propagating and self-invigorating tendency. Neither of the two is likely to exhaust itself, nor lose any of its vigour. Mixophobia and mixophilia coexist in every city, but they also coexist inside every individual city dweller. Admittedly, this is an uneasy coexistence, full of sound and fury – though signifying a lot to the people on the receiving end of the liquid-modern ambivalence.

It all started in the US, but leaked into Europe and has by now spilt over most European countries: the tendency of the better-off urban dwellers to buy themselves out of the crowded city streets on which anything may happen, of which little can be predicted, and into 'gated communities': the walled-off developments with strictly selective entry, surrounded by armed guards and stuffed with closed-circuit TV and anti-intruder alarms. Those lucky ones who have bought themselves into a closely guarded gated community pay an arm and leg for 'security services': that is, for banishment of all mixing. Gated 'communities' are heaps of little private cocoons suspended in a spatial void.

Inside gated communities the streets are empty most of the time. And so if someone who 'does not belong', a *stranger*, appears on the pavement, he or she will soon be spotted, before any damage can be done. As a matter of fact, anybody whom you can see walking past your windows or front door can fall into the category of strangers, those frightening people of whose intentions you can never be sure. Every unfamiliar passer-by may be a prowler or a stalker, an intruder with ill intentions. We live, after all, in the time of mobile telephones (not

Image Left
CCTV cameras, London, 2008

Image Right
Eastgate Street, Chester

to mention MySpace, Facebook and Twitter): friends can exchange messages instead of visits, all the people we know are constantly 'on line' and able to inform us in advance of their intention to pop in, and thus a sudden, unannounced knock on the door is an extraordinary event and a signal of potential danger.

The term 'gated *community*' is a misnomer. As we read in a 2003 research report published by the University of Glasgow, there is 'no apparent desire to come into contact with the "community" in the gated and walled area … Sense of community is lower in gated "communities"'. However the residents (and the estate agents) may justify their choices, they do not pay exorbitant rental or purchase prices in order to find themselves a 'community' – that notoriously intrusive and obtrusive 'collective busybody', opening its arms to you only to hold you down in steely chains. Even if they say (and sometimes believe) otherwise, people pay all that money in order to *liberate* themselves from company – *to be left alone*. Inside the walls and the gate live loners, people who can only tolerate such 'community' as they fancy at the moment and only at the moment they fancy it.

The majority of researchers agree that the main motive prompting people to lock themselves inside the CCTV-monitored walls of a gated community is – whether consciously or subconsciously, explicitly or tacitly – their desire to keep strangers at arm's length. Strangers are dangers, and thus every stranger is a potential danger. Or so, at least, they believe. And what they wish more than anything else is to be secure from dangers. More exactly, though, it is to be secure from the incapacitating *fear* of insecurity. They hope that the walls will protect them from that fear. The snag, however, is that there is more than one reason to feel insecure. Whether credible or fanciful, the rumours of rising crime and of throngs of burglars or sexual predators lying in ambush and waiting for an occasion to strike constitute just one of those reasons. After all, we feel insecure when our jobs, and thus our incomes, social standing and dignity, are under threat. We are not insured against the threat of being made redundant, excluded and evicted, losing the position we cherish and believe to have earned forever. Nor are the partnerships we cherish foolproof and secure. We may feel subterranean tremors and expect earthquakes. The familiar cosy neighbourhood may be threatened by being demolished in order to clear the site for new developments. All in all, it would be downright silly to hope that all those well- or ill-founded anxieties could be placated and put to rest once we've surrounded ourselves with walls, armed guards and TV cameras.

But what about that (ostensibly) prime reason to opt for a gated community – our fear of physical assault, violence, burglary, car theft, obtrusive beggars? Won't we at least put paid to *those* kinds of fears? Alas, even on that frontline the gains hardly justify the losses. As signalled by the most acute observers of contemporary urban life, even if the likelihood of being assaulted or robbed does lessen once behind the walls (though research conducted recently in California, perhaps the main stronghold of the gated community obsession, found no difference in this sense between the gated and non-gated spaces), the persistence of fear, does not. Anna Minton, author of the thorough study 'Ground Control: Fear and Happiness in the Twenty-First-Century City', takes the case of Monica, who 'spent the whole night lying awake and far more scared than she had ever been in the twenty years she had lived on an ordinary street' when 'one night the electronically controlled gates went wrong and had to be propped open'. Behind the walls, anxiety grows instead of dissipating – and so does the dependence of the resident's state of mind on high-tech gadgets, marketed on the promise that they will keep the dangers, and fear of dangers, out of court. The more gadgets one surrounds oneself with, the greater the fear that they may 'go wrong'. And the more one worries about the menace lurking in every stranger, and the less time one spends in the company of strangers, the further one's 'tolerance and appreciation for the unexpected recedes' and the less one is able to confront, handle, enjoy and appreciate the liveliness, variety and vigour of urban life. Locking oneself in a gated community in order to chase fears away is like draining the water out of the pool to make sure that the children learn to swim in complete safety.

Oscar Newman, American town planner and architect, suggested in 1972, in an article with the telling title 'Defensible Space: People and Design in the Violent City', that a preventive medicine against fear of urban violence is the clear marking of boundaries – an act that would discourage strangers from trespassing. The city is violent and teeming with dangers because – so Newman and dozens of his enthusiastic apostles and converts decided – it is full of strangers. Want to avert misfortune? Keep strangers at a safe distance. Make your space compact, brightly lit, easily watched, easily seen through – and your fears will vanish; you can savour, at long last, that wondrous taste of safety. As experience has shown, though, concerns with making space 'defensible' have led to a sharp rise in security concerns. Tokens and symptoms of security being a problem remind us of our insecurities. As Anna Minton put it in her recent study: 'The paradox of security is that the better it works the less it should be necessary. Yet, instead the need for security can become addictive.' [6] Of safety and security, there is never enough. Once you start drawing and fortifying borders, there's no stopping. The principal beneficiary is our fear: it thrives and exuberates, feeding on our border-drawing and border-arming efforts.

In the sharpest conceivable opposition to Newman's opinion are the recommendations of Jane Jacobs: [7] it is precisely in the crowdedness of the city street and the profusion of strangers that we find succour and free ourselves from the fear oozing from the city, that 'great unknown'. The short word for that link, she says, is *trust*. Our trust in the comforting safety of city streets is distilled from the multitude of minute sidewalk contacts that we make. The sediment and lasting trace of casual public contact is a tissue of togetherness-in-public woven of civil respect and trust. The absence of trust is a disaster to a city street, Jacobs concludes.

Miroslaw Balka picks up where Jacobs leaves off, achieving in one bold yet simple installation what a long line of scholars have struggled to depict in hundreds of learned and opaque books. The gate to his thirty-metre long, tunnel-like chamber is wide and invitingly open, signalling a public space. There is no light at the end of the tunnel that Balka invites us to explore. Rendered pitch-black, the interior could not be darker. Darkness is the epitome of that awesome and fearsome unknown lurking in the experience of the city. Dark space is the emptiness, the void, the naught embodied: and you may suspect that it *looks* empty only because your sight is poor, your power to pierce the darkness inadequate, your imagination failing. That sensual emptiness may be just a disguise and cover-up for terrifying corporeal content. You suspect – you *know* – that in a dark space anything might happen.

No one would therefore blame you if you hesitated to enter that darkness

A large gated community in Plano near Dallas, Texas, 2003

were you to find yourself in the Turbine Hall alone. Immersing oneself unaccompanied into that black hole of unexplored wilderness is something that only the most reckless among us, or mindlessly adventurous, would dare attempt. But fortunately, there are many people around you, all hurrying to enter. And so many people already inside! Once you go in, you'll feel their presence – not an obtrusive, harrowing presence, but soothing and encouraging – the presence of strangers, miraculously transformed into fellow human beings; a presence emanating confidence, not anxiety. When sunk in the mind-and-sense-freezing void of the great unknown, humanity is your life-boat; the warmth of human togetherness is your salvation. The streets of the 'defensive spaces' and gated communities need, ideally, to be emptied of strangers,

even if the thought and effort invested in the pursuit of this prevents you from ever forgetting your fear. The tunnel in Tate Modern's Turbine Hall is, on the contrary, tightly packed with strangers; but it is also empty of fear. Miraculously, the darkest space has been transformed into the freest zone.

Endnotes:
[1] In my *Liquid Modernity* (Cambridge and Boston 2000).
[2] Teresa Caldeira, 'Fortified Enclaves: The New Urban Segregation', in *Public Culture*, vol.8, no.2, 1996, pp.303–28.
[3] Nan Elin, 'Shelter from the Storm, or Form Follows Fear and Vice Versa', in Nan Elin (ed.), *Architecture of Fear*, New York 1997, pp.13, 26.
[4] Steven Flusty, 'Building Paranoia', in: *Architecture of Fear*, New York 1997, pp.48–52.
[5] Richard Sennett, *The Uses of Disorder: Personal Identity and City Life*, London 1996, pp.39, 42.
[6] Anna Minton, *Ground Control: Fear and Happiness in the Twenty-First-Century City*, London 2009, p.171.
[7] See her *The Death and Life of Great American Cities*, New York 1961.

Visitors inside
Lascaux II, a replica
of the original Lascaux
Grotto, France, 1983

William Daniell
*In Fingal's Cave,
Staffa* (from *A Voyage
Round Great Britain*
1814–25)
Aquatint on paper

John Warwick Smith
Grotto of Pausilippo
from *Album of Views
in Italy*
1778–9
Pencil and water-
colour on paper

CAVERNS.

Visitors viewing by
torchlight the interior
of the ice-grotto in
the Surtshellir (Black
Cavern), Iceland,
c.1860

That's How It Is

Julian
Heynen

Translated by
Fiona Elliott

Take it from here
He starts with a dead person.
By the time *Remembrance of the First Holy Communion* was presented to visitors to a small, deserted house in the country in 1985, the particular ritual associated with this right of passage was already addressing an unrecoverable past. The boy in his best suit – dressed for the transition into adulthood and standing silently bolt upright, awkwardly, hesitantly touching the edge of the table – is a fragile construction. However patiently it has been put together, the body poised on an unlocatable piece of floating ground is distinctly makeshift. Made from concrete and clay, the figure would like to persuade us of its presence. Yet all it has to back it up are flickering memories and the schematic points of information that may be gleaned from the fake reality of the photograph on the table top. The artist was once that pale boy, or he could have been; but it doesn't matter one way or the other because the situation portrayed here is a collective ritual in the place where he comes from. The picture shows what has come down to us across the treacherous bridge of memory. All we see is a shell, although with a glowing, red (fabric) heart – like a fetish – into which the guests attending the ceremony have stuck needles. This invocation of death reinforces the impression made by the figure as a piece of sculpture.

It is not by chance that it recalls those graveside statuettes which – rather than appealing to any notions of idealism or abstraction – determinedly, yet despairingly, aspire to convey an enduring, faithful image of the real form of the deceased. However much the work and the circumstances of its first appearance are concerned with the existential moment of the transition from youth to adult, from carefree abandon to responsibility – marking the passage from student to 'free' artist in Balka's own life – it is also just as much, in a more general sense, about the unavoidable frailty of memory and even more about the fact that the world we encounter is fundamentally in the past tense. As he himself once said: 'Everything we touch is coming from the past, it's our access to death.'[1]

This statement is closely tied to the place and time the artist inhabits. The main place is his own body, the main time is that in which the latter changes and ultimately disintegrates. To this day – as in his early performances from the mid-1980s and the figurative sculptures of the late 1980s which then gave way to more object-focused work – Balka's own body is always directly or indirectly present in his work, as a symbol for all bodies and as a persistent point of reference, be it in sight or not. It is not only implicit in the discreet arithmetic of his titles that describe the measurements of individual components in his works but are also related to the actual dimensions of his own body. It is also inherent in objects such as bed-like structures, points of entry and exit (reminiscent of bodily orifices), substances such as salt, ashes, hairs or even soap, and the movements of the hand-held camera in video films – all of which point to the human body as the inescapable basis of all experience, as the unrelenting condition and limitation on all our perceptions and actions. Each person's corporeality determines their fundamental consciousness of time: it is not only that the changes in their body, from day to day and from year to year, mark out a particular sequence, the body also has inscribed into it a sense of the miracle of its own beginnings and the certainty of its own end. Inextricably entwined with the place and time of Balka's corporeal form is the place, Poland, and the time since the Second World War and the Holocaust, that lengthy, in some ways still ongoing 'postwar' period. For the sculptor, Balka, this place is neither an abstract entity nor – most definitely not – an ideological construct. It is a tangible, familiar piece of the world, that is to say, the former spa town of Otwock (near Warsaw) where he grew up, its streets, squares, buildings, his grandparents' house, which he later used as a studio. 'In the yard Miroslaw Balka picks up a piece of rusty metal. It's fallen off the roof … "I can use that", he says with satisfaction, knocking the dirt off it and tossing it into his car.'[2] It is a piece of metal

from a house that a Jewish family had previously lived in. This place is the source of materials and items such as the remains of a post that was used in the fence around the Jewish ghetto,[3] or the ancient linoleum from his grandparents' house. Otwock had already sharpened Balka's response to a particular part of the past, which was evident even before more or less explicit German words started to infiltrate his exhibition titles,[4] and before he started (in about the mid-1990s) to approach places of death in his work – concentration and extermination camps.

Kaleidoscope
From the outset – and even more so in the last ten years – Balka's publications and catalogues have included not just illustrations of his works but other pictures, too, predominantly photographs or video

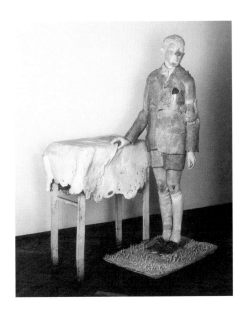

Miroslaw Balka
Remembrance of the First Holy Communion
1985
Steel, marble, concrete, silicon, textile, ceramics and photograph

Miroslaw Balka
Stills from *The Fall*
2001
Video

stills that he has shot himself. Sometimes they appear in conjunction with explanatory texts, sometimes they accompany works of art and texts in a fairly loose, associative manner. At times it seems as though their message is intentionally tucked away in tiny details obscured by the blurriness of the shot. They are obviously not primarily informative, but more about processes such as conjuring up a mood, ideas and memories or making a sudden – delayed – connection between two factors, for instance a particular work and a certain place in history. There are echoes here of the writing of W.G. Sebald who scatters similarly inconspicuous-conspicuous images into his novels and stories. However much one seeks to discover the nature of their interaction with the text, it is always impossible to fully identify it. If anything, the relationship of these images to the rest of the work could be said to provide an additional point of contact for the connection between the work and the reader, or viewer. It creates a certain amount of room for manoeuvre (only mildly directed by the artist) for the recipient's own exploration of the work and the questions it raises.

For this present book, Balka has gone a step further by including visual materials that are not of his own making, that is to say, pictures by other people, pictures of all kinds in a variety of media. The final selection of images relates to a list of words that occurred to the artist as he was working on the project for the Turbine Hall – although it is impossible to say what these words actually represent: concepts or images. Let's call them notions that can materialise in one form or another. Sometimes there was a particular event or object for which a suitable picture had to be found, sometimes the picture was already in Balka's mind's eye, where it stood for the event or object. In some instances the pictures are highly visual, in others they look like attempts to give visible form to abstract notions. Aside from their actual purpose, in this book the selection of images could also be read as a small cross-section through the history of the ongoing struggle with regard to the relations between thoughts and images. On the whole, this selection could be described as a kaleidoscope – even if strangely obscured – a splitting and faceting of internal and external images that, rather than mapping out a straight, compulsory route to some destination, open up a wide-ranging field of possibilities. However, it would be an error to interpret the artist's procedure here as in any way arbitrary. It is more of a precautionary measure on his part in view of the size and fragility of his questions, his themes. Ever alert to the risk of constraining that very open field of image-word-image connections, the following seeks to capture individual prismatic reflections that flash into view from the contact between this kaleidoscope and older works by Balka and how they possibly relate to *How It Is*.

Under the ground
There was a time when Balka always took visitors to his home in Otwock

Miroslaw Balka
34 x 34 x 27
2007
Steel, plaster

Miroslaw Balka
Still from *Narayama*
2002
Video

to see the former Jewish cemetery. Between the few surviving grave-stones, it was not uncommon to find human bones showing up on the surface of the sandy ground. In one area of the fairly hilly site, the sand had been partially removed, in all likelihood as a building material for some new houses directly behind the cemetery. Things that ought to have been sealed underground forever, in eternal darkness, far away from night and day, had been forcibly exposed to the light again – through carelessness, ignorance or sheer indifference. Forgotten. Like a distant echo of this situation, one of Balka's later works contains a sequence of stills, shown on a monitor, that appear to follow a load of sand on the back of a moving lorry (p.30). The title *Narayama* refers to a Japanese story, also told in two movies, about the enforced yet voluntary, almost ritual death of an old woman. Regardless of the story, the sand on the back of the lorry is 'used' nature, it serves particular purposes: a raw material that binds, fills, covers, buries. Elsewhere, in a short video film, the same material crops up again, this time as an apparently gigantic image. (In actual fact it is merely a close-up of a small souvenir, a toy.) Landscapes and worlds form and dissolve again, a dark, endless drama of becoming and decaying ruled by instances of falling, flowing, spilling. And then more sand, or soil, now in connection with the associative pictures that Balka has selected for *How It Is*. We see it in a photograph of Babi Yar (p.31), the gorge on the outskirts of Kiev where German troops shot over 30,000 Jews in September 1941, and where the wall of the gorge was subsequently blasted, burying the victims under tons of earth. There are even more dramatic, horrific records of the aftermath of the event than this one. However, this photograph brings out all too clearly the gulf between victims and perpetrators, between the dead and the living. Dominating the picture is the unstable wall of the gorge, at its base, rather indistinct, traces of those who have been murdered, their clothes; clearly silhouetted on the skyline, in full command of the situation, are the players in the murder. Between the two are the tons of material that were to plunge the proof of this deed, the corpses, into darkness. But that was not to last; the Soviet army later shifted the earth again, uncovering the bodies and the crime. Since then, time has reshaped the terrain yet again. Now all that remains of the gorge are some hollows in a park, although it is still the same earth. A memorial marks the place seeking to cast some light into the ever-recurrent threat of obfuscation that we call the past and oblivion. What happened here is literally and metaphorically concealed underground. Emotions, documents and knowledge penetrate this lightless place, but can never entirely illuminate it. Although the earth has yielded up a certain amount, it is still hiding so much. Balka deploys this loose, almost fluid substance in his work specifically because of its dual nature. In that sense it is also like memory: it is inconsistent, deceptive, vital to sustain life, somewhere between firm foundations and quicksand.

Housings

A soldier stands in a wide field, tired but upright; directly next to him is the entrance to his dugout, his shelter, his quarters in a hostile land. It's almost as though he were standing outside the door of his house, after work – 'this is where I live'. The inconspicuous black hole leads down into the ground, into what must be a dark, damp, confined space. It is not only that life down there is reduced to the bare minimum with regard to space, air and light, the mound of earth also isolates its occupants from the rest of the world. It has to be like that in order to provide shelter, but at the same time it means that the occupants have no control over what is happening above ground. They have to hang on down below, waiting, whatever happens outside. Life in a bunker: sheltered yet unprotected. People have also gone under ground to live, in less traumatic circumstances than warfare – digging tunnels or using and extending natural caves. There are entire settlements of this kind and important sacred institutions that for whatever reason prefer to withdraw into the 'underworld' rather than risk exposure above ground. This retreat from the light, which scarcely filters into such dwellings, the tendency to shut out the times of day and the seasons, the act of shutting one's own person into that unimaginably vast and different mass that we call Earth, allegedly ensue when life is being lived at a less developed level, when the individuals in question lack the imagination, courage or skill to fit in with and hold their own in the outside world. Thus existing under ground can be seen as the opposite of living in the world, a primitive state or a regressive act that pre-empts what normally only comes after life, the grave, whose final darkness most people want to postpone.

Image Left
A German soldier next to his foxhole during the Second World War

Image Right
Henry Moore
Tube Shelter Perspective
1941
Pencil, ink, wax and watercolour on paper

In the early 1990s, after Balka made the transition from figurative sculpture to a reduced form of representationalism, he made a number of works that can be read as minimal or rudimentary housings.[5] They are just large enough to hold him, to hold a human being. Hanging upright on a wall, just above floor level, they are reminiscent of closets or chambers, albeit with the front wall missing, as though it had been removed for demonstration purposes. A small number of partitions, double floors or small holes indicate that they are intended for specific types of use. These chambers organise the occupant's stay and existence in extremely confined circumstances. The aim is self-sufficiency, as necessity dictates, although it is not achievable. Two tent-like hide-outs, also made from raw steel, flip the minimal housing into the horizontal, thereby creating a dark, protected zone for a recumbent, crouching, or creeping figure.[6] Salt and/or ashes,

simple yet highly evocative substances, indicators of the not-present body, are used to roughly seal off the walls at ground level, as though the occupant were making him or herself at home in a precarious situation, battening down the hatches against a hostile outside world. Lastly there is a long trunk on the floor, once again just large enough to more or less accommodate a human being.[7] It is closed on all sides, but in two places small brass pipes, cut at an angle, protrude from this otherwise hermetically sealed box. Two of these, close to each other, are in the lid, at the point where one might imagine the head of anyone inside the trunk: breathing holes corresponding to the occupant's nostrils. Another small pipe, just above floor level, looks like an outlet or outflow for something no longer needed inside the space, not wanted there. With minimal, technically straightforward means, a system is suggested that implies the presence of a living organism that this

Image Left
Miroslaw Balka
Detail from *200 x 90 x 87, 3 x (Ø 26 x 39)*
1992
Steel, salt and plaster

Image Right
Miroslaw Balka
Detail from *30 x 60 x 1, 3 x (60 x 30 x 34), 3 x (60 x 30 x 11)*
1992
Steel, terrazzo, felt

trunk could have been made for. Unsettled – with their speculations on what is inside it suddenly being taken in a very particular direction – the viewer now comes upon another detail. Directly below the side outlet there is a small lid lying on the floor, containing ashes. These remains of organic life seem to be proof of what might be described as a final metabolic process; this *Dumb Box* turns out to be a coffin.[8] But is it that obvious? Is it not rather the case that in this work and the other 'makeshift dwellings' there is a strange tension, not to say dialectic, between endings and continuance, between the darkness of a non-life and the last glimmerings of a highly concentrated life? And might it not be possible to draw a fine line from the photograph of the soldier beside his dugout/home/grave to the image of Noah's ark that also appears in Balka's kaleidoscope? The 'ark' provides shelter – in pitch-black darkness, in a tiny space – for just the necessary pairs of all types of animals and the family of the man chosen to implement the survival plan, until the window and roof can be opened again after the catastrophe and the rescue vessel has fulfilled its task.[9] We learn nothing of life in this capsule during the flood, but it must have somehow been adequate.

Entering the Black Square
It did not take long before people were drawing parallels between Balka's work and the minimal art of the 1960s. The reduced, geometric forms of his sculptures that first appeared around 1990, the boxes,

panels and cylinders and the evident lessening of direct expressivity seemed to some to be in line with Minimalism. And it also seemed there could be a connection between his use of rough, old materials and Arte Povera. His apparent references to these canonic trends in Western art and the deviations from the norm that he introduced were ostensibly in keeping with the notion of postmodern art that was taking hold in the 1980s with its hybridisation of avant-gardes, which it then extended and enriched with other repressed elements. However, apart from the fact that these readings of his work either overestimated or misjudged the level of contact a young, Eastern European artist would have had with Western art before 1989, it throws a far too small-meshed, art-historical net over Balka's work. It is not by chance that he chose to include a work by Kasimir Malevich in his kaleidoscope of pictures instead. Malevich's *Black Square* 1913–15 (p.36) not only opens up a wider historical context, it also significantly taps into a view of content that is far removed from formalist comparisons and notions of linear development. This is not the place to retrace the complex reception of this early endpoint in the history of so-called abstract art. However, if research conducted in recent decades is to be believed, it would be hard to overstate either the metaphysical intention that gave rise to this painting or its debt to the tradition of holy icons. It seems likely that Balka presents Malevich's painting as a point of reference not so much for its abstraction – whatever

that may mean – as for the real, almost palpable nature of the quiescent, compact black of this representation of non-light, of a highly active darkness. Moreover, as a sculptor his main interest would not be in the notion of an almost square plane, a virtual space, but rather in the materiality that is realised in the actual paint and texture of the picture.

On the occasions in Balka's work that there are echoes of the *Black Square*, it is always in a mediated form, never as a quotation, more of a distant reflection. Nevertheless, simple, more or less isolated geometric forms – particularly rectangles – achieve a forceful, physical presence, not least when they make the step from the vertical of a picture on a wall to the horizontal of an object on the floor. It is as though Balka had secularised the form by putting it on the same level as the most obvious and ordinary thing – the ground that we stand on and move around on. These

sculptures can take the form of markings on the floor, like a threshold, or they may appear in combination with other items (p.34). They act like stop signs, momentarily halting the advance towards something else. In a recent sculpture this moment of stepping into or across is dramatically heightened with the aid of a large, rectangular plate.[10] A concealed pipe turns the platform into a kind of see-saw that you have to walk across. As you pass the centre point the other half slaps back down on the floor with a loud, alarming bang. Besides this kind of sculptural focus on the rectangle as a form, more recently Balka has also turned his attention to the customary rectangular picture in the form of video projections. Malevich's formulation is perhaps most closely echoed in the film that shows almost nothing, just an almost white wall, with the image exactly the same size as the free-standing wall it is projected onto in the exhibition space.[11] Staring at this gently but somewhat aimlessly moving image one is drawn into a meditative state, into a vegetative mode of contemplation, only for one's thoughts to repeatedly come to a grinding halt at the sheer banality of this perfectly normal wall. It prevents one's mind from travelling out into worlds beyond the image represented. The film focuses on a peripheral zone of perception and stimulates scrutiny on the margins of the physical, without ever offering one a way out. The rectangle of the image, which is seen here *vis-à-vis*, can also be laid flat as a sculpture. Some of Balka's video films are projected downwards onto a surface made of salt in a metal frame on the floor.[12]

Thus the image is virtually turned upside down, in a metaphorical sense. It is taken from the realms of distance and perspective – kindling the imagination, speculation, even illusions – and relocated in (relegated to) ordinary reality. Even if the image does not lose its illusory character, this is nevertheless an attempt to ground it, to place it on the same level as the viewer's own bodily presence.

The *Black Square* also momentarily makes itself felt in other areas of Balka's work. For instance, walking into a solidly-built passage, thoughts come to mind of the relationship of the white border with the black square

Miroslaw Balka
750 x 340 x 255 / some in some out
2005
Steel, bricks, mortar, Zeihl-Abegg ventilators, plaster

in Malevich's painting, although here one finds a black that is not so deep, for there is an exit a few steps away, and a number of fans in the ceiling emitting powerful air currents (p.37). Elsewhere a small threshold sculpture highlights the razor-sharp division between black and white in a way that sets one thinking about darkness.[13] Or should mention be made of the series of flagstones leaning up against the wall, all but one with the title and date of a different solo exhibition of Balka's work between 1985 and 2001 carved into it (p.43), a graveyard of the artist's past activities? Or the square field of ashes (p.42), just 'the thickness of touch',[14] that turns the solid monument of the *Black Square* into an ephemeral grey on the verge of disintegration? Lest there be any misunderstanding: when Balka makes use of squares and rectangles, when he more or less isolates them, his interest is not in any artistic genealogy, nor in quoting Malevich either in agreement or seeking to distance himself from him. Moreover, it makes no difference where precisely the *Black Square* crops up, whether as a point of reference for a particular work of his own, or more generally in his thoughts revolving around specific topics. However, once it has been invoked, it serves as a foil that sharpens his way of approaching these 'ultimate pictures'. His operations in an advanced realm where materials and images enter the territory of abstraction, of pure drawing or of thinking, consistently hold on to a remnant of the 'real world'. Here, too, tangibility is his main criterion.

Darkness with lights
The ninth plague, described in Exodus, was the penultimate punishment, in an escalating series, to befall the Egyptians for refusing to allow the Israelites to leave the country (p.91). The description of the darkness that shrouds the land is minimal. As the King James Bible tells us, this unprecedented event took the form of 'a thicke darknesse … which may be felt'.[15] Its impact, again described with a minimum of words, was temporarily to destroy the normal interaction between people and to condemn individuals to inaction.[14] For all the vivid detail in the accounts of some of the other plagues described in the Bible, it seems that language has met its own limits in this case. When the sense of sight is rendered useless, the sense of touch takes over; everything comes down to bodily existence. However, the dialectic of the biblical story does allow light into the homes of the Israelites.

Miroslaw Balka
196 x 230 x 141
2007
Steel, wood, electric light-bulb and motion sensor

Early on in Balka's work there is such a light, albeit in a rather surprising form. In amongst the rigid, self-sufficient elements of his first object-like sculptures there is an almost chatty found object: an old metal rubbish bin in the shape of a penguin with its beak open.[16] However, this appealingly absurd relic of equipment in a public space only appears so eloquent because of the bulb lighting up its interior. A trapped light shines out of the part that one generally would not want to look into, shedding a little light on its surroundings, like a voice. This modest, humorous instance of a dialectic of darkness and light later takes on another dimension and deep meaning. In 2007 Balka made a short corridor, one end of which is invitingly open, while the other is firmly closed off. The rhetoric of the material used in this piece – a steel frame clad with used-looking wooden boards – is something of an exception in his work as a whole. One might easily imagine this to be a found object with a very specific history. In the middle of the corridor is a naked, illuminated bulb, suspended from a cross-spar. The walls open out invitingly at one end, but it is this small but warm light that draws you into the corridor. However, just before you step into it, the light goes out; the corridor becomes a dead place. Nothing will make the light come on again as long as you remain inside the corridor. It is only when you turn on your heels and walk away that it switches back on. This piece sets up a moment of frustration. From a distance the light makes a connection with you, its life calls out to your own.

However, as soon as you pursue it, it retreats, as though the presence of one precluded that of the other. A place that puts up resistance to you, an experience that can never be had in full. Balka has not only laid a trap here, one that thwarts our urge to follow a light in darkness, he has also constructed a 'metaphysical machine' by the simplest of means.[17] In conversation he has also talked of it in connection with the notion of a near-death experience.[18] However, the corridor is far from an illustration of this particular human experience that comes to some who are momentarily clinically dead. Rather it breaks down this unseen thing – for which there are no words – into something unquestionably present. The at times nebulous accounts of these moments are specifically not translated into the ambiguity of a two-dimensional picture, into painting for instance, or into a mythologically coloured symbolic language. Instead we find a construction that is wholly open to scrutiny, a soberingly ordinary-looking construction, with a banal bulb for a light at the end of the tunnel. However utterly unsuitable this simple contraption seems to be in this context, it is only credible in this form, as a crude, poetic apparatus. It is only by making clear the endless distance between the medium and the extreme questions that he is addressing, that Balka has any hope of not entirely missing the mark. As so often, it is the details that pin down the paradox – in this case the naked electric light that always goes out when you need it most.
'… but all the children of Israel had light in their dwellings.'[20] When

darkness befell the Egyptians, interrupting life's usual patterns, there was still light in the homes of the Israelites. More or less concurrently with the corridor, Balka also made a small sculpture that sums up the paradoxical function of light sources in his work. It takes the form of a ceiling light, a petit-bourgeois version of a chandelier, although in this case the 'lamps' are made of plaster (p.30). There is no escaping an association with domestic comfort, a light that creates a feeling of togetherness. Yet the plaster lamps are in effect petrified, dead 'light' that only conveys a vague sense of its potential power. This ceiling light is a strange mixture of darkness and illumination, of warmth and cold. Its almost too familiar form is not only a sign of closeness, but also of vulnerability. This domestic item and the petrified light preserved within it is but a weak counterpart to the 'dark side of things' that Balka touches on in his work, a mere flicker compared to the works that delve deep into darkness itself. And yet, there is a 'possibility of light'.[21]

Paths into darkness

Ancient myths and the pictures of the modern era that are based on these present the domain of Hades – the shadowy realm of the dead or literally darkness, that which we cannot perceive – as a place filled with a multitude of terrors. However, it is not portrayed as just another place, as the negative of this world. Particular importance also attaches to the path to Hades, the path into the underworld marked out by the traveller's arrival at the river Styx, separating our world

from the next, the crossing of the Styx in Charon's barque, and the moment of appearing before the god Hades. The theological, philosophical and psychological meanings of this and other descriptions of the path into death are self-evident. Of necessity they resort to recognisable metaphors to explain something that has never been seen and cannot be understood. Real burial grounds, for instance those of the Ancient Egyptians or Neolithic man in Britain, also pay particular attention to the passage from this world to the next, where effort is required to make the journey from light into complete darkness. It is only relatively recently that Balka first contemplated this zone in his work, although there are earlier shades of it here and there that dissipate into the muted twilight that pervades most of his videos. More often darkness is indirectly evoked by somewhat weak lights.[22] Later on, when he coats the walls of the exhibition space with a two-and-a-half-metre high, continuous layer of ash (right), or makes a long, narrow walkway with twists and turns from simple timber,[23] although he may literally and metaphorically be working his way towards darkness, these pieces are presented in the full light of the exhibition space. Not so in the case of How It Is. As the viewer approaches, it looks like a huge container, a mighty sculpture with a powerful presence. However, walking round it brings one to something else entirely, and to a sudden halt. A fragment of memory: turning the pages of the philosopher Robert Fludd's magnum opus of 1617 the readers may find, to their surprise, a large black square taking up much of page twenty-six (p.36).[24] 'Et sic in infinitum' is inscribed into all four margins of the dark square: 'And thus into infinity', a something that one cannot imagine. The non-picture comes at the beginning of a chapter about shadows and *privatio*, a word that translates as both 'privation' and 'liberation'. Cut. The back wall of the colossal container has been lowered, forming a ramp into the darkness. What wonders or beasts await us inside? Will we have the curiosity and calm determination of János in Béla Tarr's movie *Werckmeister Harmonies* to pursue the unknown, in astonishment, or will we gaze at it from outside, uninvolved and suspicious? The steel room is large enough for its depths to be shrouded in mystery as we enter, but it is also wide enough to move about freely inside it – alone or with others. It is

not pitch black inside, just increasingly dark; turning around we can still see outside. This mise-en-scène of the unknown is overwhelming, but not because the Turbine Hall where it is placed would dwarf any smaller structure. The fact is that the mighty, raised up steel body – as tall as a house – corresponds in size to our inner sense of the unknown, of the limits of life. The effort and huge amount of material that went into making it were necessary to convey the notion, the fear, the black block that weighs us down on the last path. The sculpture had to become almost absurdly large in order to give a true sense of the threat that looms at us in the shape of the last wall in the realms of our imagination. However, when one in fact enters the black box, there is no climax to this sense of the overwhelmingly uncanny, instead there is a kind of gradual dis-illusion as one becomes accustomed to the darkness,

Miroslaw Balka
*0.5 x 2085 x 250
(The Dead End)*
2002

Miroslaw Balka
Detail from *2 x (55 x
23 x 27), 190 x 190
x 0.3*
1995
Steel, linoleum, PVC,
ash, felt

Miroslaw Balka
Detail from
+GO-GO
(1985–2001)
2001
Terrazzo, paint

an in-sight into 'how it is'. *Privatio*: deprived of the certainty of life yet also liberated from fear? The black container is a paradox. It has the dimensions of fear and is large enough to accommodate a social event, but it also has the intimacy of an individual thought and the normality of a single life. We step into a real model, a device that creates a zone just this side of metaphysics – even as I write, three months before it is finished.

In the cellar

In Balka's grandparents' house, as in many others, there is a trapdoor in the floor, indicating that there is a cellar below. It stands open, the camera shows the dimly lit start of the steps leading downwards. Quickly and in a strong voice, albeit without any particular emphasis, almost like an announcement, Balka – off-camera – enunciates the same sentence time and again into the dark opening: *Dlaczego w tej piwnicy nie ukrywaliscie Zydow?* Like a bland litany. Every second time, endlessly, he switches on an extra light, although it does not cast any additional light on the situation. The question goes unanswered, not by the relatives who once lived here, nor from the depth of the cellar, nor by the one who is asking: 'Why didn't you hide any Jews in this cellar?' So it has to go on being repeated. That's how it is.

Endnotes:

[1] Iwona Blazwick, 'Interview', in *Possible Worlds*, exh. cat., ICA and Serpentine Gallery, London 1990, p.18.

[2] Hanna Krall, 'Das Haus', *Da ist kein Fluß mehr*, translated from Polish by Roswitha Matwin-Buschmann, Frankfurt am Main 2001, p.143.

[3] *97 x 38 x 45, 1942–2006*, in *Reflejos condicionados*, exh. cat., Fundación Botin, Santander 2007, p.19.

[4] Such as *Rampe* (1993), *Winterhilfsverein* (1994), *Selection* (1997), *Lebensraum* (2003).

[5] Such as *50 x 40 x 1, 190 x 50 x 40, 190 x 50 x 40, 190 x 50 x 40*, 1992, in Julian Heynen (ed.), *Bitte.*, exh. cat., Museum Haus Lange, Krefeld 1992, fig.2.

[6] Also, see *203 x 79 x 93, 191 x 65 x 7, 190 x 6.5 x 11* 1992, in *Privacy: Luc Tuymans/Miroslaw Balka: 1958–1998*, exh. cat., Fundaçao de Serralves, Porto 1998, p.69.

[7] *190 x 60 x 54, Ø 9 x 1* 1992, in exh. cat., Krefeld 1992, fig.7.

[8] *Dumbox* is the title of a work made by Joseph Beuys in 1982.

[9] Genesis 6:14.

[10] *250 x 215 x 25, 30 x 7 x 25* 2006, in *Nothere*, exh. cat., White Cube, London 2008, pp.60–4.

[11] *The Wall*, exh. cat., London 2008, pp.76, 96–7.

[12] Such as *T.Turn* 2004 (exh. cat., London 2008, p.88), *The 3rd Eye* 2006 (*Lichtzwang*, exh. cat., K21, Dusseldorf 2006, p.29).

[13] *60 x 30 x 4, 60 x 10 x 4* 1994, in *Winterhilfsverein*, exh. cat., Moderna Galerija, Ljubljana 1994, fig.1.

[14] (the thickness of touch) As cited in Caoimhin Mac Giolla Leigh, 'The Light Gleams an Instant', in *Miroslaw Balka, Tristes Tropiques*, exh. cat., Irish Museum of Modern Art, Dublin 2007, p.42.

[15] Exodus 10:22, 21.

[16] 'They saw not one another, neither rose any from his place for three days', Exodus 10:23.

[17] *Penguin Lamp* 1990, exh. cat., Dublin 2007, pp.65, 67.

[18] 'The possibility of light. A conversation piece', Miroslaw Balka, Julian Heynen, Juan Vicente Aliaga, Santander, 26 July, 2007, 12am, in exh. cat., Santander 2007, p.122.

[19] Ibid.

[20] Exodus 10:23.

[21] For this and the next quotation, see note 18.

[22] As in, for instance, *Shepherdess* 1989 (*Die Rampe*, exh. cat., Van Abbemuseum, Eindhoven and Museum Sztuki, Lodz 1994, p.30), *250 x 196 x 164, 190 x 89 51, Ø 10 x 15* 1994 (exh. cat., Eindhoven / Lodz, fig.2) or *Eclipse* in the Kröller-Müller Museum, Otterlo 2001.

[23] *190 x 90 x 4973* 2008, exh. cat., London 2008, p.75.

[24] Robert Fludd, *Utriusque cosmi maioris scilicet et minoris Metaphysica, physica atque technica Historia*, Oppenheim 1617–1719.

Miroslaw Balka
Still from *Dlaczego*
w tej piwnicy
2007
Video

45

Miroslaw Balka's list
of references for
How It Is, April 2009

How It Is (Totems)

Plato's caves

Are they?

30 × 10 × 13 =

3900 m³

PH
ZB
JMC
    L.K.
      JH
        HS.

.Strangers are dangerous...

..on velocity

Caves

Holes

Babi Jar

to APH
4 imes from A.

2,10666
3900 : 1800
36
30
180
180
180

2,10666

Shells

Noah's Ark

Noe's Ark

navels

Whale

Hell visions

— Memling
Blake etc

Malevicz

Black Holes

Hades

FOX
Fox
holes.

Courbet
Origine
du Mond

plague
of
Darkness
(Doré)

Ufo

Space ship Appollo

Open
graves

Big Black vibrator

Leviathan

Jack the Ripper

Dark corner
Dangerous Place

Kain

Uboot submarine

Mecca

Jonasz   Jonah

15×12
  ×10
1800 m³

Kaaba

Hadiar

my cellar entrance ←

same Treblinka Stangl?

Bernard Picart
Scene of Hell
1731
Engraving

Anonymous (after
Andrea di Cione
Orcagna and
Francesco Traini)
Dante's 'Inferno'
c.1460–70
Engraving

The Illuminating Darkness of *How It Is*

Paulo
Herkenhoff

1. Ramp, box and darkness

How It Is consists of a ramp, a large steel box and darkness. In rational terms, 3,900 cubic metres (30 x 10 x 13 m) is the volume of darkness it contains. Measurements have always concerned Miroslaw Balka in his work, but *How It Is* is irreducible to its external form and dimensions; it is a sculpture to be experienced from the inside and in the absence of light. Rendered black, this internal physical zone has not otherwise been mediated or filled by the artist.

In the course of preparing this exhibition, Balka made a rough list of his sources – references to people, books, myths, historical facts, artworks and other triggers for his thinking that provide clues to the possible analysis of the many strata of meanings in this work. This essay takes Balka's list as a guideline, while acknowledging that it is a minefield, a dangerous seduction under a regime of austerity.[1] The question is: how, precisely, do these annotations illuminate *How It Is*? Clearly, the work should not be taken as a mirror, a paradigm, a metaphor, a replication or an illustration of any of these hypotheses. They are not cited to induce precise visual correspondences; nor is Balka making an Erwin Panofsky-like study of iconology. The list is not an attempt to establish the reality or truth of *How It Is*, which is irreducible to a univocal interpretation. Indeed, its main function might be to assert that criticism will always fall short of the many possible perspectives for the analysis of an artwork, which, like the *Relational Objects* of Lygia Clark, continuously change focus depending on circumstance, context, and the subjectivity of the participant.

Instead, Balka is simply offering a vast history of darkness, a layering of connections, concepts and facts, sources and references that are devoid of hierarchy and that propose conjunctions of personal and historical memory; these may range from the cellar in his studio in Otwock, to a Suprematist painting by Kasimir Malevich, to Plato's cave, to Joseph Conrad's *Heart of Darkness*,[2] to the Ka'ba and to cosmic black holes.

When considering Balka's list of references, it should also be remembered that Ernst Cassirer's *animal symbolicum* might not survive in *How It Is*.[3] Balka both resists and embraces the reduction of references to the process of symbolisation; he tests the relativity or even the inutility of symbols through the transitivity of meanings of the referent, refusing to establish a formal grammar or a fixed lexical grouping. He does not embark, for example, on orthodox equations between the lack of light and the morally debased or the spiritually lost.

The sculpture draws on an unexpected glossary of darkness to create a minimal and alternative semantic articulation of the language of darkness. Its palette of darkness is a poetic project to reconcile reason and imagination in concrete contexts. As in other works in his oeuvre, the physical structure of *How It Is* disorients accepted social and political systems. To decipher darkness is to understand the concepts, values and facts that are enunciated in *How It Is*, a porous structure that absorbs subjective processes like the fear of the uncontrollable and the unknown. Balka evokes in this work the *différend*, that concept developed by Jean François Lyotard to analyse conflicts of discourse, contradictory

and yet equally legitimate, with no universal rule of judgment that could resolve the dispute. Refusing a totalitarian solution, *How It Is* becomes an invitation to thinking in terms of a 'discontinuous form'.[4]

When contemplating the outside of this structure, basic questions arise: is it a pavilion, a piece of architecture, a room, a box, or a geometric solid? *How It Is* may have the external appearance of a geometric building, like, for example, Etienne Boullée's spherical *Cénotaphe de Newton* 1784, but inside the structure, these appearances no longer apply. Darkness provides no reliable dimensions. It dislocates the visitor to the realm of the immeasurable and should be thought on the level of innumeracy, heard as the unutterable, seen as the formless, lived as an

Étienne-Louis
Boullée's design for
Newton's Cenotaph,
1784
Ink and wash
on paper

anxious territory without etiology, and sensed without boundaries. Balka is proposing a phenomenological situation that demands an understanding of the psychoanalytic dimension of the subject within a social equation. *How It Is* acts in the confrontation between vision and language, between darkness and the 'ill-said'.

Darkness is Balka's language for what has been silenced or 'ill-heard'. It is a cut in reality. It acts as the vibrant signifier of the unsayable, of the socially obliterated, of what has been placed under a process of visual disappearance, of what lacks language. Balka does not wish to conjure the sublime in this work; the urge is to approach the unconfigurable, the unrepresentable. The porosity of meanings and symbols, the lack of spatiality and the visible brought about by Balka's sculpture creates a lack that is potentially perturbing for an art audience.

'*How It Is* is about the layers', says the artist.[5] His condensed net of allusions provides a wide range of stimuli, both physical and conceptual. This text therefore remains open to the conceptual permeability of his oeuvre and the complex set of references that charges the static darkness with a dynamic material force. His many ideas will be tested in this essay in the interpretation of his polymath artwork within the context of science, philosophy, phenomenology, psychoanalysis, history, religion, mythology, theatre, architecture, literature and art, as well as Balka's personal experience.

Balka's list constructs a transversal history of darkness. The totalising and universal perspective of art history is a battlefield that can become a device for the obliteration and exclusion of artists, art movements, whole cultures and differences. For this reason, this text will refer to some less canonical artists, and in particular to Cildo Meireles, who as a Brazilian artist can be seen as belonging to a peripheral society similar to Balka's Polish context. Balka knows that in spite of dramatic changes in the last three decades, art history remains a Western enterprise, and maintains a Eurocentric discipline rephrased in the post-war years by a dislocation of focus to the United States. *How It Is* cites this European legacy, including the Christian vision of Hell presented by Dante, Hans Memling, William

Miroslaw Balka
Black Pope and Black Sheep
1987
Wood, carpet, textile, steel, paint

Blake and Gustave Doré (in *The Plague of Darkness*, c.1866). Guy Debord writes in *Society of the Spectacle* that 'capitalist production has unified space, which is no longer bounded by external societies' and 'this society which eliminates geographical distance reproduces distance internally as spectacular separation'.[6] *How It Is* shows an awareness of this centre-periphery dichotomy in global capitalism: darkness is paradoxically the same and different everywhere. Balka takes the discipline of art history as a field of metaphorical condensation and metonymical fragments and presents an alternative history that defies boundaries and shortens distances. Art history is a battlefield against the Derridean *mal d'archive* and the obliteration of artists, art movements, whole cultures, and differences.

Like the 'rustle of language', an expression coined by Roland Barthes,[7] Balka proposes a linguistic shift, a semantic inflection and a syntagmatic grouping of references to be breached in all directions. The semiological approach in this essay on the language of darkness involves ambivalences, polyvalences and paradoxes in the linguistic expression of darkness through disjunctive references. Balka's hallucinatory range of references in *How It Is* indicates a dynamic, and probably endless, process of semantic accretion of meanings. Thus he plays in this work both with the mutability and the immutability of the sign of darkness to describe it as a place that drives the visitor towards knowledge.[8]

As Jacques Derrida has written, the metaphor of darkness and light (of self-revelation and self-concealment) is 'the founding metaphor of Western philosophy as metaphysics'.[9]

2. Invisible mirrors

In his milestone study of post-war daily life, *Mythologies* (1957), Roland Barthes demonstrates how Ferdinand de Saussure's vast system of sign analysis can be extended to the level of mythology. Since myth is discourse, he argues, everything can be myth.[10] As a dominion of pure darkness inscribed in the museum, *How It Is* makes reference to the shadowy abode of Hades, the Greek god of the Underworld. Balka's intertextual weaving also articulates ideas from Plato's *Republic* about representation, mimesis, mirrors and the gaze. Thus *How It Is* can be seen as a work that calls for a contemporary reactivation of the meaning of mythology.

This approach falls into the context of many different generations of artists who have referred to myth and fable: Louise Bourgeois (the existentialist Sisyphus), Joseph Beuys (the mythological quality of honey in *How to Explain Paintings to a Dead Hare* 1965), Francis Bacon (the carnality in *Triptych* 1976, related to Aeschylus's play *Prometheus Bound*), Anna Maria Maiolino (whose *Between Lives* 1981 establishes a tension between the pre-verbal and the non-verbal in the cycle of life and death with reference to Demeter), Kara Walker (allusions to Leda in gender violence against the body under slavery), Matthew Barney (Pan in *OTTOshaft* 1992), and Kendell

Geers (the confrontation of Eros and Thanatos), among others.

Hades received from Athena a polished shield (*Aegis*) that functioned as a mirror. He was also given the Helmet of Invisibility to fight the war against the Titans (*Titanomachy*); hence Hades is the 'unseen' (in Greek *Haides* or *Aides*). This game of optical instruments in the story of Hades forms a link with *How It Is* in terms of visual perception.[11] The exhibition visitor's experience of *How It Is* is a paradoxical one, in which one is pitilessly confronted with absolute invisibility – of the Other, one's environment, and even of oneself. *How It Is* assures that in the absence of light, the viewer is deprived of 'mirrors', without which the Self no longer occupies a position as the static centre of visual experience.[12] Once inside *How It Is*, one's inability to see in the dark generates a perceptual loss, so that one's entire experience is subjected to a semiological dissolution. In this way, Balka inverts the modern function of art: rendering visible. The task of *How It Is*, conversely, is rendering invisible. In his work, visitors experience a state of topographical agnosia. They must use senses other than vision to navigate the internal space. Isolated in darkness, the visitor experiences a semantic wandering, where objects, places, names, people, forms, sounds lose meaning. The less we see in real darkness – the more perfect that darkness is – the more transparent its concept becomes. In this way Balka shapes

the lexical meaning of darkness into its textual meaning in history.

The concept of *How It Is* makes reference to Book X of Plato's *Republic*. Here, Socrates refers to the craftsman (painter/poet) as 'Him who makes all the things that all handicraftsmen severally produce ... this same handicraftsman is not only able to make all implements, but he produces all plants, and animals, including himself, and thereto earth and heaven and the gods and all things in heaven and in Hades under the earth.'[13] While the craftsman can create 'everywhere and quickly', others could do so only if they 'should choose to take a mirror and carry it about everywhere'. But, goes the counter-argument, the craftsman's representation is unsatisfactory, since he would produce 'the appearance of them [all things], but not the reality and the truth'. Thus Socrates excludes the creator from the Republic as a liar. But as A.R. Goodrich has warned, insufficiently analytical interpretations of Plato's ideas can lead to an unjustifiably reductive reading. Plato's address to the artist's deficiency in disseminating reality could be seen as 'advancing a new aesthetic', instead of constituting an attack on the arts.[14]

Balka constructs *How It Is* in order to discuss the ancient Greek theory of form presented by Plato, including the origins of painting, departing from a dialogue on optics and pictorial illusion and moving to the conversion of the visible into painting. In the dialogue *Cratylus*, the same Plato who sought to assign the correct status to painting in the *Republic*, discusses linguistics, including the etymology of Hades, the unseen.[15] A discussion of the unseen requires raising the opposite concept of *eidos*: that which is seen. Again, mythology turns *How It Is* into the construction of the unseen.

Applications of Jacques Lacan's theory of the 'mirror stage' to contemporary art have become a plague. Balka is well aware of this platitude, but these ideas have obvious validity here. Related to the myth of Narcissus, the mirror stage is a step in the development of an infant that occurs between the ages of six and eighteen months, when the child becomes captivated by his or her own image. Lacan, who first described his theory in 1936, assigns a double value to the mirror stage: 'it marks a decisive turning-point in the mental development of the child'and 'an essential libidinal relationship with the body image'.[16] In 1949, Lacan again deemed it relevant to focus on the mirror stage: 'for the light it sheds on the formation of the *I* as we experience it in psychoanalysis'.[17] The infant experiences 'a flutter of jubilant activity' in regarding his specular image, and, though limited by undeveloped motor skills, assumes a sense of his body as 'total form' and a symbolic matrix of the primordial force of the *I* (the ideal-*I*). In *Seminar IV*, Lacan adds that 'the mirror stage is far from the connotation of a mere phenomenon which presents itself in the development of the child. It illustrates the conflictual character of the dual relationship' between the Ego and one's own body in specular format, and between the Imaginary and the Real.[18]

How It Is also offers a 'flutter', but in this case of doubt, a rupture in the laws of the Gestalt perceptions that rule our understanding of our own exteriority. *How It Is* denies mirrors to all Narcissuses and proposes the ill-recaptured. Instead, the ego is confronted with a *méconnaissance* (misunderstanding) in the gaps between the Imaginary and the Symbolic. There is no place for the mirror when the subject is engulfed in darkness. There is dissonance between perceiving one's own specular image and the control of one's bodily motor skills, between capturing the wholeness of the body and the self-perception as a fragmented body.[19]

The Lacanian discussion of heteromorphic identification ('the question of the signification of space for living organisms')[20] can be applied to visitors to museums. 'The symbolic order', writes Lacan, 'is present in the figure of the adult who is carrying or supporting the infant. The moment after the subject has jubilantly assumed his image as his own, he turns his head round towards this adult who represents the big Other, as if to call on him to ratify this image'.[21] In the symbolic language of *How It Is*, the adult is the artist, who cares for the visitors wandering under his asymbolic regimen of blind mirrors.[22]

3. Allegory of shadows
How It Is can also be taken as part of

a culture of shadows and opacity that includes sciagraphy and shadow theatre. In *Vision, Reflection, and Desire in Western painting*, David Summers asserts that 'the foundational myth of European painting is about light and shadow'.[23] He points out that *skias*, from *skia* (shadow), also means 'shade, canopy, pavilion'. This can be applied to the double level of experience in *How It Is*: the structure is both pavilion (*skias*) and shadow (*skia*).[24] Summers adds that in Homer's description of Hades, a ghost of the dead is usually called 'psyche' or 'eidolon' but may also be called 'shadow' (*skia*). In Greece, *skiagraphia* was the art or science of representing shadows found in nature as accurately as possible, most notably by the 'shadow painter' (*skiagraphos*) Appolodorus of Athens. Balka can be seen as a 'shadow sculptor', delineating the silhouettes of viewers.

This sciagraphic dimension of *How It Is* adduces notions of loss and desire. In China, shadow play (*pí yˇɪ ng xì*), a form of storytelling, was created for Emperor Wu of Han (156 BC – 87 BC) after the death of one of his concubines; it aimed to bring her back to life. Barthes has described a neoclassical narrative tracing the birth of painting, which tells of the love-struck daughter of a Corinthian potter who reproduces her lover's silhouette by drawing the outline of his shadow on a wall.[25] The sculpture of the skiagraphic Balka is what Leonardo called *via di levare*, but is a form revealed through the gradual absence of light and not through the suppression of mass.

Image Left
Cildo Meireles
*Blind Mirror
(Espelho Cego)*
1970
Wood, mastic, metal

Image Right
Miroslaw Balka
sza
1999
Newspaper,
glue, steel

The physical structure of *How It Is* cites the discussion between Socrates and Glaucon in the *Republic* where Plato presents the allegory of the cave to discuss the extent to which human 'nature is enlightened or unenlightened'.[26] This is a crucial epistemological question for Balka in his inquiry into the realm of the visual. The importance of a conceptual understanding of darkness as such is enlightening, but his process in *How It Is* refutes any actual insertion of physical light. This is Balka's apparent paradox.

To quote Socrate's description of the cave:

Behold! human beings living in an underground den ... here they have been from their childhood, and have their legs and necks chained so that they cannot move, and can only see before them, being prevented by the chains from turning round their heads. Above and behind them a fire is blazing at a distance, and between the fire and the prisoners there is a raised way; and you will see if you look, a low wall built along the way, like the screen which marionette players have in front of them, over which they show the puppets ... And do you see ... men passing along the wall carrying all sorts of vessels, and statues and figures of animals made of wood and stone and various materials, which appear over the wall?

Socrates questions the prisoners' interpretation of the shadows on the wall as men passing by with different objects, asking if what they see is in fact only their own shadows, thrown by the fire on the opposite wall of the cave.[27] Thus Plato's allegory speaks of the confrontation between levels of enlightened and unenlightened nature. He concludes: 'the prison-house is the world of sight, the light of the fire is the sun, and you will not misapprehend me if you interpret the journey upwards to be the ascent of the soul into the intellectual world'.[28] Plato thus posits the conflict between the world of the senses (the cave) and the world of ideas.

Visitors to *How It Is* could feel like Plato's prisoners, yet they are not imprisoned in darkness by Balka. In Plato's den, one prisoner escapes; leaving the cave means meeting the sun, light, the world, knowledge of the real. Conversely, it is on entering the den of *How It Is* and confronting darkness that one encounters the real. *How It Is* is the empirical resolution, through art, of the philosopher's proposition of conflict between Form and Ideas. Menaced by the deprivation of his sense of vision, the viewer is situated by Balka in the very *locus* of visual reasoning. The process of 'disenlightening' leads to the acceptance of the conflict between the indescribable and unmeasurable form and the concept of darkness. Thus Balka extends Plato's warning that without philosophy ordinary viewers are like the prisoners in the cave. Higher speculation is needed and that is the task of art – art being a practical space for experiencing the world, as philosophy was for Plato. Further, Balka refers to the distinction between the invisible and the intelligible made by Plato.[29] In *How It Is*, Balka inverts Plato's assertion that only the real is invisible to establish that 'only the invisible is real'.[30] For him, the loss of light is no longer a metaphor for the inaccessibility of knowledge, but rather, an epistemological possibility.

4. Pneuma

In its modesty and formal severity, *How It Is* is a stoic object. No emotional appeal is staged. Even when compared to the exoskeleton of a shell, *How It Is* has no affinity with that 'painted skeleton' put forward as a metaphor by Friedrich Nietzsche in *The Wanderer and his Shadow* for 'those authors who would like to compensate with artificial colouring for what they lack in the flesh'.[31] Balka considers his work 'a sculpture, yes, a situation too, but definitely not architecture or an installation'.[32] He refutes the intellectual seduction of mapping the formless, the reification of nothingness, the vulgarisation of the uncanny or a logocentric filling of the void. Thus his work is more a shelter for and in darkness.

A sculpture whose main substance is air and darkness recalls the many definitions of *pneuma* posited by the Stoic philosophers. For the Stoics there is no empty space; everything is constituted of *pneuma* – breath or soul – seen as the *causa continens* (sustaining cause) of all living bodies. In this respect, *pneuma* is substantial matter. A soul, says Aristotle, 'is substance in the sense which corresponds to the accounts of a thing'.[33] Inside *How it is*, especially

for those agitated by the absence of light, this human vitality is experienced as hyperactivity. The 'breath of life' coincides with the primal darkness.

To the Stoics *pneuma* is enabled by a state of *tonos* (tension) determined by the combined dynamic activity of *hexis* (holding), *physis* (nature), *psyche* (mind or soul) and *logica psyche* (rational mind or soul). These four elements are the active forces of air and fire, distinct from the passive character of water and earth. Gradations of *pneuma* are dependent on the proportion of fire and air. The *pneuma* may take the form of a vegetative life force (*physis*), animal life force (*psyche*) and the soul of rational beings (*logica psyche*). In this sense, the *pneuma* acts to conform the human being and endows him with qualities such as thought and judgement.

From this perspective, Balka infuses *How It Is* with that pulmonary *tonos*. As a metaphorical lung the structure provides an inner *pneuma*, which holds darkness in equilibrium and separates it from the world. But the relationship of Balka's oeuvre with the notion of *pneuma* or the soul ends here. His art is not subordinate to religion nor imbued with a spiritual sense. This does not mean that he is not concerned with the essential signs of human life, but that his interest lies more with the phenomeno-logical experience of individuals.

For Aristotle *pneuma* is connected to a pre-respiratory life force, the transmission of a soul from parent to offspring.[34] He saw the vital heat of

Diagram illustrating
Plato's allegory of the
cave, from Ed Miller's
*Questions that Matter:
An Invitation to
Philosophy*, New York
(2008 edition), p.71.

semen as the embodiment of the soul. The primal circumstances in the life of the new born were emphasised by the Brazilian art critic Mário Pedrosa before he shifted his focus from Gestalt theory to the phenomenology of perception as propounded by Edmund Husserl and Maurice Merleau-Ponty: 'in the first day of birth, children already make a capital differentiation. They perceive a luminous point in darkness. The world no longer presents itself confusedly to them as chaos, as a diffuse entanglement of sensations, but rather as a delimitated field, over which a figure is noticeable. And everything organizes itself around this structure.'[35] *How It Is* touches on that vital and extreme need for light in original darkness. Balka's sculpture calls to mind Constantin Brancusi's *Newborn* 1915, a truncated ovoid that touches the world at just one point of its surface. This point of tension in *Newborn*, which is that affective 'luminous point in darkness', corresponds to the *punctum* in which visitors find themselves in *How It Is*. It is a site of gravity and the dislocation of tension to another form of perception. It makes visitors aware of the presence of the human body under the laws of physics. The viewer regresses towards that first day of differentiation and contact; every notion of structure, either temporal or spatial, is dissolved. *How It Is* substantiates darkness and disembodies art. This primal tension inside the work becomes a diagram of social tension in the cultural institution.

*5. Noah's Ark: of measures
and collections*
Balka cites Noah's Ark as a reference point for *How It Is*. 'This is how you shall build it', God told Noah: 'the length of the ark shall be three hundred cubits, its width fifty cubits, and its height thirty cubits'.[36] The cubit is an ancient measure based on human anatomy (the length of the arm from the elbow to the tip of the middle finger), and Balka has often used his own bodily dimensions in his works. For the 1993 Venice Biennale, for example, he created *Soap Corridor* – a passageway in which a 'wainscot' of soap was installed at the level of the artist's own height – as well as *37.1 (Cont.)*, lastrico slabs electrically heated to the temperature of the human body.

'Of every clean animal, take with you seven pairs, a male and its mate; and of the unclean animals, one pair, a male and its mate', God further instructs Noah.[37] Technically, the Ark was a floating museum of living specimens. The content of *How It Is* is solely darkness. Thus *How It Is* and Noah's Ark share museological problems of collecting. If Noah's Ark needed an extraordinary extension of

space to house its collection of animals, the challenge for the internal structure of *How It Is* was how to shelter the incommensurable asset that is darkness. As a consequence, the only feasible unit of measurement for *How It Is* is that taken from the extended forearm of visitors in their primal effort to situate themselves in a space without light and to walk around securely in this flood of darkness.

In a sense, *How It Is* is a container for an absent art collection – a *musée imaginaire* – whose empty darkness evokes references that include Jonah, Thomas Hobbes's *Leviathan*, Hades, tombs, photography, the camera obscura, Christian visions of Hell as in Dante's '*selva oscura*',[38] Memling, Milton, Blake, Doré, the Tabernacle and the Ka'ba.

As Lacanian signifier the body of darkness of *How It Is* can contain a collection of synonyms to build a dissonant collection of terms: murky, darksome, darkling, tenebrous, sombrous, nocturnal, caliginous, sombre, dingy, umbrageous, benighted, Erebus, adumbration, obumbration, obfuscation, zero, sciagraphy, gloom, lightlessness, blackness, colourlessness, noctivagation, obliteration, Shoah, praying, lying, the unconscious, Freudian slips, dreams, scotophobia, nyctophobia, nyctalopia … But although *How It Is* is a quasi-museum, darkness cannot be collected or archived.

A collector himself, Freud stated that: 'a collection to which there are no additions is really dead'.[39] This relating of collecting to death was echoed in Freud's own biography, since he started to collect after his father had passed away. Balka's work too has made a correlation between accumulation and death. His exhibition *sza* (*Hush*), named after the last three letters in the Polish word for silence, *cisza*, took place at the Galeria Foksal in Warsaw (p.56). The space was festooned with paper chains made from newspaper obituaries stuck together with bone glue. A hole in one of the windows gave the gallery a deathly chill.

The piece *750 x 340 x 255 / some in some out* (p.37), installed in the Italian Pavilion at the Venice Biennale in 2005, was a concrete corridor with five ventilators in the ceiling that created a claustrophobic passageway for the flow of cultural tourism, recalling the bleak historical architecture of oppression under the Communist regime that Balka experienced in Poland. (He had been referring to his Catholic upbringing in post-1945 Poland since his early piece *Remembrance of the First Holy Communion*) In the Turbine Hall, visitors are led into the space of *How It Is* via the ramp at Tate Modern, a museum architecture that absorbs and controls the fluid dynamics of hoards of visitors. Architecture is always an integral part of Balka's work. 'The dialogue with existing architecture takes place on some levels and is as important as other layers', says Balka. His works devised for specific sites 'could be shown in different places and attempt a dialogue with other architectural situations. The first

presentation is like being born, the other if it takes place, is like changing places in life. That's why the relation with the ramp at Tate Modern is only one element.'[40] In other words, Balka's works enter into a state of semiotic mutation that establishes their intertextuality. His museological choices – site-specificity, darkness, slipperiness, wind, temperature – are uncollectable and institution-resistant materials.

Balka installed *Cruzamento* (2007, p.64) in front of the entrance of the Museu de Arte Moderna do Rio de Janeiro, an open area that leads to the ocean. He placed the cruciform steel net structure in accordance with the museum's orthogonal relation to the nearby airport, thus establishing another crossing. The horizontal upper beam of the cross pointed towards the main hall of the museum and the lower towards the offices. The left arm pointed to the bay, and the right to the city. *Cruzamento* evokes the Crucifixion. It fuses Polish Catholicism, a seedbed in Balka's oeuvre, with the pathos of the Iberian High Renaissance and Counter Reformist ideas. Other site-specific references are the gigantic statue of *Christ, the Redeemer* 1938 on top of the Corcovado peak in Rio, a statue attributed to the sculptor of Polish descent Paul Landowski; and the Southern Cross constellation, visible in the Southern hemisphere and represented in the Brazilian flag. *Cruzamento* is open to the light, transparent and breezy. Like *750 x 340 x 255 / some in some out*, it contains five electric fans, placed at intervals along its length, so that the viewer experiences a strong current of air while crossing through it. Thus, like *How It Is*, though empty, *Cruzamento* refutes the baroque *horror vacui*. It contains zones of air. The fans stand for the Five Holy Wounds of Christ during the crucifixion. Its austerity runs counter to the drama found in historical representation of this subject, such as El Greco's *Ecstasy of Saint Francis* or *Saint Francis receiving the Stigmata* c.1575–80 (p.65), which was discovered in 1964 in the church of Kosow Lacki, which, as Balka has pointed out, is very near to Treblinka. This creates a certain sense of parodic inversion. Balka understands the potential force of ironically subverting his references, as evidenced in the equally austere *How It Is*, whose location in Tate Modern provokes expectations for the presence of art.

The allusion to stigmata made by *Cruzamento* also refers to the mystical rapture in *Ecstasy of Saint Theresa* 1652, the marble group by Bernini in the Cornaro Chapel of Santa Maria della Vittoria in Rome. In her *Life Written by Herself* (1565) Teresa Davila reveals her ecstatic vision, where an angel appeared to her:

He had in his hand a long spear of gold, and at the iron's point there seemed to be a little fire. He appeared to me to be thrusting it at times into my heart, and to pierce my very entrails; when he drew it out, he seemed to draw them out also, and to leave me all on fire with a great love of God. The pain was so great, that it made me moan; and yet so surpassing

was the sweetness of this excessive pain, that I could not wish to be rid of it. The soul is satisfied now with nothing less than God.[41]

As they walk through *Cruzamento*, re-enacting the Via Crucis, the souls of visitors are touched by the air from the fans, a play on the Greek concept of *pneuma* in the sense both of 'breath' and 'soul'. The sensual bodily pleasure they experience inverts the wounds represented by the fans into a source of refreshment and delight.[42] Similarly, some scholars interpret Bernini's version of Teresa's ecstasy as an orgasmic state instead of one of divine joy. Freud's term for human processes that 'have no apparent connection with sexuality but which are assumed to be motivated by the force of the sexual instinct' was *Sublimierung* (Sublimation).[43] This concept of *Sublimierung* can also be applied to the artistic process. *Cruzamento* and *How It Is* are devices for parodying both the notion of the sublime and of sublimation.

6. Transparent darkness
In their depiction of workers alienated from the product of their labour, Karl Marx and Friedrich Engels stated in *The German Ideology* (1846) that 'the production of ideas, of conceptions, of consciousness, is … directly interwoven with the material activity and the material intercourse of men, the language of real life'.[44] All mental production, they argue – including art – dialectically originates from the material behaviour of men. In this context, they compare ideology to optics: 'if in all ideology men and their

circumstances appear upside-down as in a *camera obscura*, this phenomenon arises just as much from their historical life-process as the inversion of objects on the retina does from their physical life-process'.[45] Seen in these terms, *How It Is* unveils alienation. In this work, where Balka turns to Malevich's Suprematist zero degree of form and its reductive aesthetics,[46] he takes the viewer to the limits of Theodor Adorno's 'end of philosophy' and Fredric Jameson's 'end of art'.[47]

In the Marxist metaphor, the infra-structure (the economic base) supports the super-structure (the legal-political and ideological levels). The Lacanian Louis Althusser sees ideology as a representation of imaginary relationships with the real world. The museum is a cultural version of Althusser's 'Ideological State Apparatus (ISA)',[48] which the philosopher situates between the base and the superstructure. The interior of *How It Is* is an uncommodified zone. Darkness resists capital accumulation. As the raw material and final product of *How It Is*, it implies neither use value nor exchange value. It allows for no economic operations, no personal possessions, no museum collection. Thus the distributive mechanism of the capitalist system fails.

Lyotard asks whether 'interlocutors are victims of the sciences and politics of language understood as communication to the same extent that the worker is transformed into a victim through the assimilation of his or her labor-power to a commodity?'[49] For Marx, 'capitalist production is *essentiellement* the production of surplus-value'.[50] *How It Is* embraces antagonistic strategies of non-commodification and non-accumulation. Althusser compares Marx's concept of ideology to the imaginary construction of dreams. Slavoj Žižek has argued that 'ideology is not simply a "false consciousness", an illusory representation of reality, it is rather this reality itself which is already to be conceived as "ideological"'.[51] He asserts that, according to Lacan, 'Marx "invented the symptom" (Lacan) by means of detecting a certain fissure, an asymmetry, a certain "pathological" imbalance which belies the universalism of the bourgeois "rights and duties"'.[52] The theoretical framework of Althusser and Žižek allows for the notion that *How It Is* refers to the order of the unconscious.

Balka's economy exposes art as aggregated value. As darkness overcomes the schism between use value and exchange value, *How It Is* deviates from the model of the 'desiring machines' of Gilles Deleuze and Félix Guattari. The disjunction in the signifying chains, a Lacanian concept, establishes that the materiality of the sign is insignificant here. 'Isn't the support completely immaterial to these signs? The support is the body without organs.'[53]

Worthless darkness is Balka's ironic play on the logics of financial capital. In this sense *How It Is* equates to the face value of Cildo Meireles's *Zero*

Miroslaw Balka
Cruzamento
2007
Steel, air ventilators

El Greco
The Ecstasy of Saint Francis
1577–8
Oil on canvas

dollar bill 1978–84, which clarifies 'the gap between exchange value and use value, or between symbolic value and real value.'[54] Both artists operate the imaginary constitution of the art object as a sign-exchange value. Balka agrees with Jameson that 'the image is the commodity today'.[55] The darkness inside How It Is, like the act in Lygia Clark's Caminhando (Walking 1963),[56] is a material sign with neither surplus value nor exchange value. It suggests taking the performance of temporal surplus value in the organisation of social time. It performs a tentative disclosure of ideology critique applied to itself without becoming the final self-destruction envisioned as a rational critical potentiality.[57]

7. Camera obscura and the white cube
Light, not darkness, is the widely accepted symbol of knowledge – as Dante describes it in the Inferno: 'rays of the planet that lead us straight on every path'.[58] However, the absence of light in How It Is does not stand for what Dante called 'the silence of the sun'[59] – or for an epistemological collapse. Balka takes no such route from light into darkness, or the other way around, as a measuring table of the process of knowledge. In America: A Prophecy, William Blake, who is quoted by Balka in relation to How It Is, refers to an antithetical 'Demon's light' as a form of celebrating contradictory states.[60] The transfer of certain findings from science into art does not mean a clash of paradigms. Balka respects science, yet his art is irreducible to an illustration of scientific laws and hypotheses.

The physical form of How It Is could be interpreted as a gigantic camera obscura: a room-sized box that operates as an optical device. When light from a scene passes through a hole in the camera obscura, it strikes a surface where the image appears upside down with accurate perspective. The camera obscura is, of course, one of the inventions that led to photography, a medium that Susan Sontag, in the first pages of her On Photography (1973) compared to Plato's cave.[61] 'The photograph is literally an emanation of the referent', writes Barthes in Camera Lucida: Reflections on Photography.[62] Seen in the light of Barthes's proposal, How It Is can be interpreted as an etymological emblem of the language of photography (from the Greek phos, meaning 'light', and graphe, representation through lines, i.e., 'drawing') – imago lucis opera expressa (image revealed by the action of light). As a working instrument for painters, the camera obscura is also part of art history. Leonardo da Vinci described it in the Codex Atlanticus. Vermeer, Canaletto, Reynolds and Ingres are among the painters who made use of it.[63]

From the mid-nineteenth century, the camera obscura was developed in structure, format and design to become known as the 'black box'. In this sense, the camera, and photography itself, can be seen as a container of Leviathan appetite, recalling Blake's vision in The Marriage of Heaven and Hell in which the monster's 'mouth & red gills hang just above the raging foam tinging the black deep'.[64] Balka's 'black box' also evokes the ideas of the philosopher and phenomenologist Vilém Flusser, who, in order to define that monstrous appetite, traces the etymology of 'apparatus' to the Latin verb *pareparare*, in the sense that an 'apparatus' is a device that lies in wait: 'The photographic apparatus lies in wait for photography; it sharpens its teeth in readiness.'[65] Flusser's consciousness of the possible alienating implication of the photographic apparatus (as an invention to simulate specific thought processes) and Balka's awareness of the museological machine, take the two on convergent strategies. Viewers wander inside the darkness of *How It Is* much as Flusser describes the wanderings of photographers 'inside' the camera: 'It is exactly the obscurity of the box which motivates photographers to take photographs', says Flusser, 'They lose themselves, it is true, inside the camera in search of possibilities, but they can nevertheless control the box.'[66]

Another possible approach to *How It Is* is to take it not as a camera obscura, but as a scotoma, or blind spot – an obscuration of the visual field instead of a manifestation of the Cartesian optical gaze. A scotoma, or *punctum caecum*, results from the lack of light-detecting photoreceptor cells on the retina or optic nerve. In *How It Is*, there is no light to activate these photoreceptive cells. Balka choses not to operate within the retinal system, creating instead, in an almost Duchampian manner, a physiological scotoma by introducing

his black box inside the white cube of the museum. In this sense *How It Is* acts as false *camera lucida*,[67] a negative prism that refracts light *in absentia*. Inside this 'blind spot' the viewer experiences enlightenment.

The 'viewer' navigates through the darkness of *How It Is* in a search for a possible vision and re-empowerment of the gaze. In order to orient themselves in this phenomenologically limitless space, they must find the centre in themselves. A parody of 'the white cube', Balka's institutional critique turns off the light. The 'white cube' becomes the shadowy region for a pilgrimage of perception. In *Inside the White Cube: The Ideology of the Gallery Space*, Brian O'Doherty remarked that we have now reached a point where we see not art but the *space* itself first.[68] 'You are there without being there.'[69] Inside the white cube, argues O'Doherty, 'the sanctity of the church, the formality of the courtroom, the mystique of the

Box reflex camera obscura, 1845–55

experimental laboratory join with the design to produce a unique chamber of esthetics.'[70] *How It Is* brings the spectator out of this limbo-like atmosphere promoted by the ideology of the white cube gallery in a symbolic reversion of the language of the art system and the power conveyed through museological space.

8. Scientific darkness

How it is appears much larger from the inside than from the outside. Other sculptors, such as Anish Kapoor in a work like *Void Field* 1989, employ light and colour to provide the same sensation as one looks inside the holes carved into the stone. Thomas McEvilley called this 'darkness inside a stone', a metaphysical place 'inside the mind, not the space of the ego'.[71] In *The Poetics of Space* Gaston Bachelard speaks of a dimension of 'intimate immensity'.[72] In Balka's work one might talk of 'unmeasurable immensity', where substantive darkness cannot be mistaken for an absent sign. The semiotic referent (real darkness) is complemented by the comparable measurability of the geometric exterior of the signifier (30 x 10 x 13 m).

As referents to his own body, dimensions are important in Balka's works and are often used as titles, such as *188 x 40 x 52, 42,5 x 13 x 2,5* 1992 and *2 x (190 x 60 x 80)* 1994. However, in *How It Is* there can be no correspondence to the dimensions of the artist's own body, since darkness is immeasurable. The dimensions of *How It Is* have more

in common with the Ka'ba (15 x 12 x 10 m), the ancient sacred stone building towards which Muslims pray, situated in the centre of the Grand Mosque in Mecca, Saudi Arabia, and which houses the sacred relic *Hajar-ul-Aswad* (the Black Stone). Yúsuf Alí comments that Abraham and Ismaíl built: 'The Ka'ba as the house of God / And purified it, to be a center / Of worship for all the world.'[73] Just as the phenomenological depth and grandiosity of darkness in *How It Is* goes far beyond the apparent external and objective limits of 3,900 cubic metres, the volume 1,800 cubic metres cannot account for the immeasurable spiritual immensity of the Ka'ba.

The discrepancy between one's perception of the external and the internal dimensions of *How It Is* can be juxtaposed with the notion of 'number' in the Minimalist oeuvre and theoretical constructs of Mel Bochner. Husserl's famous assertion 'Go to the things themselves' is crucial to Bochner's phenomenology of Minimalism. In his article 'Serial Art, Systems, Solipsism' (1967), Bochner refers to Carl Andre's arrangement of units 'on an orthogonal grid by use of simple arithmetic means', to Dan Flavin's 'progressional procedure', and to seriality based on 'numerical or otherwise predetermined derivation (progression, permutation, rotation, reversal)' in the work of artists like Eadweard Muybridge, Sol LeWitt, Donald Judd, Robert Smithson, Hanne Darboven, Eva Hesse and Dan Graham.[74] To those who consider these works to have no poetry or power, Bochner answers that 'their boredom may be the product of being forced to view things not as sacred but as they probably are – autonomous and indifferent'.[75] Externally, Balka's structure dialogues with Bochner's Minimalist forms, but on the inside follows a direction of its own. *How it is* makes clear that darkness cannot be reduced to a numerical identity, even to its basic dimensions, since on the inside it remains a body of wider, even limitless, darkness.

In *The Foundations of Arithmetic*, the mathematician Gottlob Frege concludes that: 'There is nothing more objective than the laws of arithmetic'.[76] but that these laws 'are not really applicable to external things; they are not laws of nature. But they are certainly applicable to judgments that are made about things in the external world: they are laws of the laws of nature'.[77] Balka blurs the laws of arithmetic by replacing any sense that the viewer may have of the dimensions of the space with a sense of disorientation.

A similar disruption of mathematical logic takes place in Cildo Meireles's *Fontes* 1992, shown at Documenta IX. For this installation Meireles produced 6,000 yellow carpenter's rulers in four combinations of number and measure: (1) with the numbers in the correct order and the spaces marked off at the correct distances; (2) with the numbers in the correct order and the spaces marked off at the incorrect distances; (3) with the numbers in the incorrect order and the spaces marked off at the correct distances; and (4) with the numbers

in the incorrect order and the spaces marked off at the incorrect distances. Meireles's immediate reference is Marcel Duchamp, whose text 'Idea of Fabrication' clarifies how chance and allusion to non-Euclidean geometry are behind his work *Three Standard Stoppages* 1913–14: 'If a straight horizontal thread one meter long falls from a height of one meter straight on to a horizontal plane twisting as it pleases it creates a new image of the measure of length'.[78] Meireles's work *Virtual Spaces: Corners* 1967–8 also mocks non-Euclidean geometry to establish a space that is beyond the logic of perception in order to invent virtual space and illogical topologies such as 'vertical horizons'. Both Meireles and Balka produce deregulating devices that set up a play between art and science.

For Balka, darkness is an idea, as much as a number is an idea for Frege.[79] Scale and proportions become pure impossibility. Thus darkness, as the internal dimension of *How It Is*, introduces a state of innumeracy, a situation where the viewer experiences an inability to deal with a practical notion of number or of geometry, as if he or she had suddenly become mathematically illiterate.[80]

In Husserl's *Origin of Geometry*, *modus ponens*, a topic in pure logic, is employed to prove new theorems from old ones without having to go back each time to the initial axioms and postulates.[81] Geometry, says Husserl, 'must have arisen out of a *first* acquisition, out of first creative activities'.[82] *How It Is* builds a critical approach to Euclid's original language of geometry. The loss of measurability in both the works of Meireles and Balka re-signifies space and leads to the loss of the ideality of geometry. Yet, it is not abstraction for which Balka strives when creating this friction with the tenets of science, but simply the pragmatic and symbolic experience of darkness. The work acts as an allegory of the failure of metrology in respect to the artistic experience.

Meireles and Balka also share a common astrophysical language that alludes to black holes and dark energy. Meireles's installation *The Red Shift* 1967–84, a series of three red rooms that play with modes of perception, refers to intergalactic gas clouds, while he has compared his installation *Eureka/Blindhotland* 1970–7 to the density of the accumulated energy in black holes.[83] In the model of theoretical physics, *How It Is* would be comparable to thermodynamic blackbodies, objects that absorb all the electromagnetic radiation that falls on them. At Tate, the body of darkness installed by Balka could be seen as having absorbed all art and all people. *How It Is* also raises a comparison with the black hole, since both have an invisible interior. The gravitational field of a black hole is so powerful that nothing can escape its pull. This idea of a body or mass of darkness whose interior is a dynamic space-time continuum pervades *How It Is*. Balka's work offers an 'event horizon' that can be penetrated by 'objects', including people, but out of which nothing can come.[84] Balka takes the

Miroslaw Balka
145 x 180 x 50, 123 x 150 x 42 , 29 x 28 x 29 + Two Lights
2003
Steel, MDF, leather, video

concept of the black hole in order to address the symbolic generative energy of darkness. Under this conception, *How It Is* is a field of darkness, a diagram of the collapse of energy and entropy in progress. The entropic model relies on the notion of information under agency.[85]

'Unattainable exactitude' was the unifying concept of Balka's exhibition *Element der Exaktheit* (Element of Exactitude, 2003, see above), where precision was deliberately frustrated by the discrepancy between the exact measurements defined by the titles of the works and their actuality, which deviated from this, if only in incalculably minute and hardly perceptible ways. The planned failure in these works resulted from the perverse use of optical and luminous processes such as opacity, excessive luminosity, misaligned images, the damaging of a projected image through daylight, blurring and inaccuracy. In one work, for example, a luminous disk evoking the moon was projected onto a circular hole in a bed-like object, but the two never coincided exactly. This deregulated lunar orbit operates an inverted notion of the sublime that is close to Longinus, who suggested the terror of a world without top or bottom.[86] As exactitude is overruled, the gaze is drawn to that Borges-like fissure between the immeasurability of the infinitesimal and the finitude of life. In this sense, *How It Is* could perhaps have been included in *The Encyclopaedia of Ignorance: Everything You Ever Wanted to Know about the Unknown*, together with the solar interior, the riddles of gravitation, or why we are unable to understand pain.[87]

9. Poetics of place

The writings of Gaston Bachelard provide a philosophical ground for the basic aspects raised by Balka's poetics of everyday experience and domesticity. The dangerous spaces in Balka's oeuvre – dark corners, holes, graves, shells and caves – as well as the 'unmeasurable immensity' referred to above, could be taken partially as a response to Bachelard's *Poetics of Space*, which proposes 'a general theory of the imagination'.[88] Laying significant stress on the paradigms put forward by Bachelard, in which he applies phenomenology to architecture, stressing the lived experience of a space, Balka

establishes his own phenomenological approach to places, including graves, Treblinka, or the museum itself.

Often quoting Bachelard, Lucy Lippard has argued that 'place' is a space of memory.[89] Darkness retains little memory of time and space. Indeed, it engenders a crisis of memory. The philosopher Tzvetan Todorov warned against the unspeakable threat of effacing memory by totalitarian regimes at the end of the last century.[90] Balka's meta-darkness recalls that political obliteration of memory. The agnosia engendered by *How It Is* does not necessarily mean loss of memory. The work is more properly a metaphor for visitors adrift in the museum, submitting to the regulating model of art history. However, the piece is directed less at peripatetic bodies than at sharply imaginative minds. *How It Is* can thus be placed within the conceptual framework of *imagination matérielle* (material imagination) and *volonté matérielle* (material will) introduced by Bachelard in *La Terre et les rêveries de la volonté* (Earth and the Reveries of Will, 1949). His suggestion that matter reveals our forces and that material reality instructs us has been an inspirational idea for materialist discourses on art, influencing a wide range of post-war artists including Yves Klein in France, Louise Bourgeois in the United States (in spite of her contradictory evaluation of Bachelard's philosophy), Victor Grippo in Argentina and Hélio Oiticica in Brazil. In *How It Is* Balka expands Bachelard's concept to propose an unsolved conundrum: darkness sustains an *immaterial* will.

Darkness evokes the fearful imaginary places of childhood memory. Balka's poetics of spaces of horror, resistant to the sublime, recalls Louise Bourgeois's explorations of childhood guilt and abandonment. The uncanny domesticity of his early life in Otwock pervades his oeuvre.[91] In the exhibition *Betong/Concrete* at Malmö Konsthall with Antony Gormley and Anish Kapoor, for example, he simulated the concrete walls of his childhood home. He has spoken of the 'dark corner', 'dangerous places', 'my cellar entrance', adding that in his work 'there are relationships between my body and the room, between myself and the corners'.[92]

The Bachelardian phenomenology of the corner resonates in Balka's work. In *How It Is*, the imaginary dark place is condensed into the actual space, where the corners of the room are dangerous and where the solitude, in Bachelardian terms, 'negates the Universe'.[93] Emily Dickinson's lines: 'The Brain has Corridors – surpassing /Material Places' resonate in the space of *How It Is*,[94] where darkness is erected as part of the affective architecture of the subject. As a body with a menacing imaginary of 'dark corners', *How It Is* can be interpreted as a house. 'Our house', Bachelard argues in *The Poetics of Space*, 'is our corner of the world', the 'house of the Being'.[95]

In *Introduction to Psychoanalysis* Freud describes the pathological dread of the dark, 'nyctophobia' (from the Greek *nyx* 'night' and *phobos* 'fear'). In connection with this he recounts the following anecdote: 'I once heard a child who was afraid of the darkness call out: "Auntie, talk to me, I'm frightened." "But what good will that do? You can't see me;" to which the child replied: "If someone talks, it gets lighter"'.[96] Balka has described his own nyctophobia in similar terms: 'Maybe that's why I like to get to sleep with the radio on, especially when someone is talking, not music … And because of this in the night I listen to the worst ultra-right Catholic Polish program: because it's about the waves of words not about their chemical ingredients.'[97]

The participating visitor to *How It Is*, actually a nyctalopic non-viewer,[98] takes the role of Freud's frightened child. Where vision fails, any talking, any sound, makes the interior space lighter and tames fear. For Balka, neither darkness nor art poses a threat that is commensurate with the fear of it. With an eye on Barthes, Balka aims to extract from darkness the Duchampian 'infra-slim' and Barthes's surreptitious 'rustle of language'.[99]

In ancient mythologies, shells were a symbol for the human body. Bachelard too, argues that 'the human body … encloses the soul in an outside envelope, while the soul quickens the entire being, represented by the organism of the mollusk. Thus … the body becomes lifeless when the soul has left it, in the same way that the shell becomes incapable of moving when it is separated from the part that gives it life.'[100] Balka's poetics of imagination does not mirror those of the philosopher, for it is both layered with a personal metaphor and launched in a critical confrontation with the fabric of contemporary culture. In his early days, a cannibalistic Balka spoke of a 'primeval hunger for a body. After some time I satisfied my hunger for the form of the human body'.[101] The hunger for a body in *How It Is* is that longing for the presence of the viewer. Without this presence, the work would be a lifeless shell, the body without the Bachelardian molluskular soul, a museum room without art. Thus, once again, Balka constructs with darkness the inverted metaphor of life as light.

Jaromir Jedlinski has observed that since Balka's work *Good God* 1990,

signs, traces, dimensions, temperatures, crystallised substances, used materials, sounds and aromas have replaced bodily representations in his oeuvre. 'The body is gone – what remains is corporeality.'[102] His earlier works like *Remembrance of the First Holy Communion* had incorporated the sacrament of the Eucharist and the issue of transubstantiation into the body of Christ. Leibniz has described the Eucharist as the baroque sacrament of the folded soul.[103] The etymology of 'baroque' stems from another molluskular image: *barroca*, the 'imperfect pearl' in Portuguese.

In darkness, the body loses any representational property: you are darkness or the void in you. You are the hole. There is 'always a fold on

Stalactites and Stalagmites in Carlsbad Caverns, New Mexico, c.1940

the fold, a cavern in the caverns', writes Deleuze.[104] *How It Is* is you. Lacan discusses the 'creation *ex-nihilo*' through Martin Heidegger's image of the vase that is built by the potter around a central void – a form that is created out of the hole. Like the vase, Woman signifies the hole out of which man can fill in his world. As the hole, Woman can represent 'the existence of the emptiness at the center of the real that is called the Thing,' affirms Lacan, not without stressing the role of the phallus and castration.[105] In *How It Is*, the viewer explores his *ex-nihilo* time and territory in the museum.

In these Lacanian terms, *How It Is* converses with Anna Maria Maiolino's *Black Hole* 1974, a paper structure mounted in a frame-box that reveals tears and holes. With this work, she evokes the signifier of the cut, of the void, and the Lacanian lack (*manque*). Maiolino's penumbrous artworks represent the state of exception during the Brazilian dictatorship of 1964, the capitalist counterpart to the Soviet regime in Poland, which is always recalled by Balka. For both artists, language replaces impotence. The association of holes with darkness gains the political density of a sign of mourning. 'So many holes or ravines in Eastern Europe were used by *Einsatzkommandos* as graves', says Balka.[106] It is not 'fashioning' the world *ex-nihilo*, but reducing mankind to the absolute ethical void. Both *How It Is* and *Black Hole* are metaphorical dim places of resistance against the gravitational collapse of freedom. Both can be compared to Max Bill's ideas for *Monument to the Unknown*

Political Prisoner 1952 (London, unexecuted), which proposed a cube traversed by a tunnel in search of transparency and light. All three works activate the geometric economy of light, turning the concrete 'abstract' space into a place of censorship and death but also of silent hope for transformative knowledge from the field of the unnamable real.

The symbolic speleology (study of caves) in *How It Is* can be compared to that of *Cavern of Anti-Matter* 1959 by the Situationist Giuseppe Pinot-Gallizio, and *Cavemanman* 2002 by Thomas Hirschhorn. As Frances Stracey has noted,[107] these works were responding to the Cold War and the bombing of New York's Twin Towers on 11 September 2001 respectively, addressing in the former case 'nuclear annihilation' and in the latter, 'global terrorism'. According to her analysis, Gallizio's cavern is 'a critique of functionalism' and its 'disease of banalization,' epitomised by homogenised architectural units designed by Le Corbusier.

In fact, the structure of *How It Is* is close to Le Corbusier's designs for *pilotis* – columns used to lift buildings above an open ground level. It was a feature employed by the architect for some of his major projects in Paris, Rio de Janeiro, and New York. Le Corbusier's *pilotis* houses had a direct impact upon Louise Bourgeois's *The Blind Leading The Blind* 1947–9, initiated after she met the architect in New York in 1946.[108] The *pilotis* in Bourgeois's works are historical precedents for *How It Is*, which is a cave on top of *pilotis*, with darkness rather than Bourgeois's blindness as its cavernous interiority.

The *pilotis* were not a new invention. Adolf Max Vogt has affirmed that Le Corbusier had studied the archaeological finds of Ferdinand Keller, who from 1853–4 had excavated remains of prehistoric houses that had once been lifted above the water level of Lake Zurich by pile-work stilts.[109] Balka's architectural structure at the Tate thus connects with the pillared houses on the prehistoric Zurich lake and with Le Corbusier's Villa Savoye of 1928. He invents nomadic visitors of darkness wandering in asynchronicity at the extreme edge of space.

10. Sexuality in darkness
'I am the Tenebrous – Bereft
  – Disconsolate,
The Prince of Aquitaine, his
  tower ruined:
My sole star is dead
  – and my constellated lute
Bears the Black Sun of Melancholia'
– Gérard de Nerval, *El desdichado*
(The Disinherited)[110]

The lightless sun of Gérard de Nerval, his imagery of depression, leads us to associate *How It Is* with a pervasive image of personal and cultural impasse – 'the black sun of melancholia'. Melancholia has pervaded Balka's works, including *Fire Place* 1986 (p.107), where the focus is a dismembered torso inside a furnace built in brick. Obituary notices are pasted on the outside, while a rectangular opening is

occupied by a light bulb, which gives light and warmth. Thus life, death and mourning circulate in a single space. In this way, Balka addresses himself to the unconscious – using ideas of brightness and darkness as a way of sublimating and convoking desire.

The combination of the torso and the opening in *Fire Place* points to Gustave Courbet's *L'Origine du monde*. This painting is a cut-off image of a woman's torso with fully exposed genitals. Here, the erotic gaze enters the dark cave of the female body. As Jack Lindsay has argued, in *L'Origine du monde*, Courbet transformed human organs into a landscape: 'the vagina forming the cave-entry, the water-grotto, which recurs in his scenes'.[111] In *The Monumental Impulse*, George Hersey claims that 'the human race has long had a penchant for using the penis as an architectural paradigm.' He develops his 'penis paradigm'[112] to analyse obelisks and towers, claiming that allusions to erections 'express specific facts about territory, generic

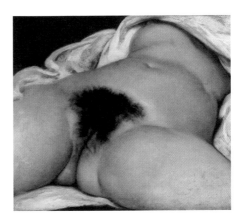

Gustave Courbet
L'Origine du monde
(*The Origin of
the World*)
1866
Oil on canvas

inheritance, and status' in architecture.[113] Prominent examples of phallic monuments that he cites are Boullée's *House of Pleasures* of 1790, his phallomorphic project for a brothel in Montmartre, Norman Foster's 'Erotic Gherkin' in London and Napoleon's column in Place Vendome in Paris. Hersey also denotes a typology of female architecture, which includes vaginal fountains and buildings and breast-like domes. He claims that 'probably the earliest of all architectural interiors are the natural caverns that Paleolithic humans filled with art. This grouping of canals, tunnels, pools, and biomorphic chambers, with their shifting levels and contrasting spaces, strikingly evoke the complexity of the female interior anatomy – as do their darkness, their fluids, their oozing walls, and their redolences.'[114]

Balka uses no such direct figurative or anthropomorphic anatomical solutions to ascribe a psychological level to *How It Is*. In fact, he builds his minimalist sculptures with no thought of the genetic homologies appointed by Hersey. However, he does inscribe the topic of sexuality in other ways. *How It Is* shares with Lygia Clark's *The House is a Body* 1968 and Louise Bourgeois's *Femme-Maison* 1946–7 or *The Destruction of the Father* 1974 an interest in geometric cellular architecture that opens as a penetrable body. The economical Balka also raises issues of desire in architecture in such a way that brings him into agreement with Adolph Loos, who asserted both

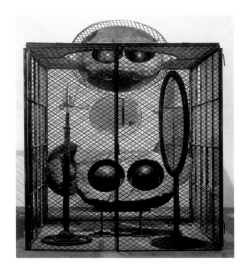

Louise Bourgeois
Cell (Eyes and Mirrors)
1989–93
Marble, mirrors, steel, and glass

that, 'ornament is crime' and that 'all art is erotic'.[115] *How It Is* becomes sexually charged through Balka's reference to Courbet's picture but also to Freud's *Totem and Taboo*. It could therefore be seen to belong to the order of provocative architectures in psychoanalytical discourse – the producing-machines, desiring-machines, schizophrenic machines listed by Deleuze and Guattari in *Anti-Oedipus: Capitalism and Schizophrenia*.[116]

In *De Rerum Natura*, Lucretius describes birth as a process of reaching the light: 'when nature, after struggle, tears the Child out of its mother's womb to the shore of light [*in luminis ora*]'.[117] Gordon Lindsay Campbell comments that *in luminis ora* 'is an epic phrase describing birth as the crossing of the boundary from dark to light.'[118] This association of darkness and light with the woman's body is suggested in *How It Is*, which although not anthropomorphic, makes reference to feminine anatomy. Balka's own 'architecture parlante' (speaking architecture) contrasts with the explicitness of *L'Origine du monde*. His is a three-dimensional response to the confrontation of desire with the *place* and the *source* that appears in two dimensions in Courbet's picture.[119]

It is revealing to picture *L'Origine du monde* among the personal belongings of Lacan, who was the owner of the work from 1953. Lacan's wife, Sylvia asked Masson to paint a panel to conceal the explicit nudity in the painting, just as the original collector, the Turkish diplomat Khalil-Bey, had a curtain made to cover it. For *How It Is* Balka does not wish to 'protect' the image of the vagina from the gaze. He rather creates an ambivalent flux of

veiling/unveiling within the gaze through the viewer's exploration of the space of shadows and darkness. He enunciates sexuality in his sculpture signifier whilst making it clear through his use of a geometric solid that the sexual is not the genitals. The process of desublimation in *L'Origine du monde* leads Žižek to affirm that the illusion of traditional realism 'lies in the belief that behind the directly rendered object is the absolute Thing'.[120] The material dimension of darkness in Balka's work offers no certainty of wholeness, synthesis, autonomy, duality, or similarity.[121]

'The painting is certainly in my gaze, but I, I am in the painting', said Lacan.[122] Perhaps a visitor to *How It Is* could paraphrase Lacan by saying that darkness is inside the gaze, but

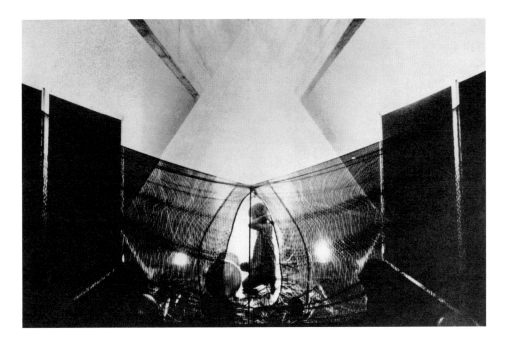

Lygia Clark
The House is a Body. Penetration, Ovulation, Germination, Expulsion
1968
Mixed media

Petrus Gilberti
'Jonah in the Mouth
of the Whale' from
*La Bible Hystoriaulx
ou les Hystoires
Escolastres*, early
fifteenth century

he, he is in darkness. He is the owner, the collector, and the interpreter. The ocular angle taken by Balka is Lacan's theory of the scopophilic regime (the sexual pleasure of looking). The cyclopic eye is the dark cave of *How It Is* and the genitals of *L'Origine du monde* that stare at the viewer and try to capture him.

11. Ecce aedificium, ecce expositio[123]
The monster that swallows up and vomits out the viewer recalls Jonah's anthropoemic whale. This term was used by Claude Lévi-Strauss in *Tristes Tropiques*, where he compared two strategies for dealing with Otherness and the Other: anthropoemy and anthropophagy (cannibalism).[124] Anthropophagous societies, he argues, swallow up, metabolise and incorporate the symbolic energy of the Other. Anthropoemy on the other hand comprises expulsion, isolation, 'separation, confinement, and barring of all contact between one people or culture and another'.[125] (Lévi-Strauss's terminology is based on the Greek *phagein* – to eat – and *emein* – to vomit.) In *How It Is*, Balka entwines this need to neutralise and incorporate differences through the anthropophagic process of entering the work, with the anthropoemic urge to be expelled from the 'whale'.

The biblical monster inspired Thomas Hobbes's *Leviathan* 1651 which proclaims that Man is evil: 'homo homini lupus' (man to man is an arrant wolfe). In response to Hobbes, Balka asks if 'artist to viewer is an arrant wolfe?' The viewer's will to leave the darkness of his sculpture is the wish to be vomited from its belly. In order to solve problems of surveillance in prisons, Jeremy Bentham devised the panopticon in 1785.[126] In his model, small windows in a tower at the center of a circular prison house allowed surveillance of all cells. This simultaneous visibility guaranteed efficient control over prisoners and guards. The prison system can act as a micro-physical diagram of power that relates to other institutions, such as the museum.[127] From the anthropomorphic perspective, the mouth of *How It Is* becomes an all-seeing eye. It is a dark panopticon that stands for the museum in general as an institution to control the spatialisation of people and art through marketing and consumption.

'We cannot escape museums … We cannot simply walk out and exit', claims Donald Preziosi. 'To avoid being eaten by a museum is admittedly a universal problem.'[128] Not coincidentally, the platform leading into *How It Is* takes the form of a rectangular apron, or tongue, thrusting out into the space of the Turbine Hall, a format that recalls performance spaces like Shakespeare's Globe Theatre, built in 1599. The apron serves as the passage of the viewer to the internal stage of *How It Is*. For Martin Herbert the semiotic activation of the body in the works of Balka 'requires a certain degree of stagecraft'.[129] The opening of *How It Is* at the top of the ramp, looks like a misplaced *vomitorium*, the passage situated below or behind a row of seats in an amphitheatre, through which crowds can 'spew out' at the end of a play. The isthmus of the fauces (the limits between the mouth cavity and the pharynx) of this institutional mouth of *How It Is* is the museum turnstile, the device for counting visitor-consumers at the museums' entrance. The hyperbolic opening of *How It Is* (10 x 13 m) may bring about the appearance of a Pantagruelian swallowing and speaking mouth when installed in the museum. This notion of Rabelaisian abundance conveys the exaggerated expenditure in Gargantua,[130] and only a Gargantuan appetite would engulf the mob of museum visitors in blockbuster shows. Laughter is an 'element of knowledge' in Rabelais, says Mikhail Bakhtin citing L.E. Pinsky.[131] This laughter is internal, not external as it might seem. Balka, like Rabelais, occupies a position beyond satire. Like Chris Burden in *Samson* 1985, Balka subverts the notion of the sanctity of museums. In Burden's installation a 100-ton jack is connected to a gearbox and a turnstile at a museum. Every visitor to the exhibition must pass through the turnstile and each time they do so the turnstile slightly expands the jack, which pushes large timbers against the museum walls. Ultimately, *Samson* could destroy the museum building but the movement is imperceptible to the naked eye. *How It Is* recontextualises this parody of the history of museum power. There is no expenditure of energy and yet the sculpture subverts, it asks for a certain disregard of the critical difference in the work because viewers have to invent their own loss of light to create another way of looking.

12. Heart of Darkness

In his poem *The Little Black Boy* William Blake introduces the problematics of 'racial' identity: 'And I am black, but O! my soul is white.'[132] Frantz Fanon approached similar issues in his *Black Skin, White Masks* of 1952, which deals with the introjection of inherited colonial values into the colonised society. 'The native bourgeoisie', writes Fanon, 'which comes to power uses its class aggressiveness to corner the positions formerly kept by foreigners'.[133] As a post-Fanon artwork, *How It Is* cannot simply be counterposed against Blake's racist antagonism between a white soul in a black body. Balka negotiates other radical turns. His sculpture represents the passage of the white cube gallery into the camera obscura, from architecture into optics.

Balka has strategically chosen to install *How It Is* at Tate Modern on the banks of the River Thames, the geographic point of departure for Joseph Conrad's narrative. This recalls Roni Horn's description of the Thames in *Still Water* – 'The river is a tunnel with an uncountable number of entrances'[134] – a statement that has resonance with both the itinerary of Charlie Marlow, the storyteller in Conrad's book who travels into the heart of Africa in a steamship, and for the visitor to Balka's sculpture. The correlation between light and place in *Heart of Darkness* affects our reading of *How It Is*. The discussion now moves from nyctophobia to agoraphobia – a fear of unfamiliar places, or of leaving 'the 'safe place'. Just as Marlow wishes to visit 'darkest Africa',

'Sketch map showing the principal journeys of the Rev. Geo. Grenfell in the Congo region & co.', 1908

so *How It Is* provides no security of light or spatial orientation.

Conrad developed a glossary of metaphors for darkness that could be an original paradigm for the mode of layering darkness in *How It Is*. From London to Congo, Marlow establishes an itinerary of different shades of light. The book starts with Marlow finding 'the most blank' space on the map of Africa, which then becomes 'a place of darkness', a metaphor for a ruthless racism and colonial exploitation.[135] Applying these ideas to *How It Is* demands a continuous dislocation back and forth from phenomenology to politics. Furthermore, Balka's reference to *Heart of Darkness* is not a straight-forward application of Dante's image of the 'savage journey',[136] but the experience of wandering through a territory irreducible to a map. The critical language surrounding colonialism is doomed to fail and evokes hesitation. Horn advances a riposte to Balka: 'Isn't that what you'd expect? Isn't that what you'd be after – to lose your identity? The Thames looks like a solvent for identity, doesn't it?'[137]

In *Heart of Darkness*, the ivory collector Kurtz had taken over tribes and waged war on others for their ivory. Near death, his last desire is to remain within the native society and he displays this through tribal fires, dance and darkness. That symbolic loss of ivory can be linked to Chinua Achebe's description of the violence of the colonial enterprise upon peoples 'who had been knocked out silent by the trauma of all kinds of dispossession'.[138] Olu Oguibe describes the importance of this 'significant silence' as the difficulty of utterance in Conrad's book: 'though this silence is not literal, it is nevertheless made palpable, for in the arena of engagement between the One and his Other, between the dominant subject and the object of his interrogation, beyond the preferred narrative and that specified rhetoric that reiterates palatable constructs of Otherness, the native's utterances are not speeches.'[139] From those perspectives, *How It Is* implies a metaphorically significant silence. The work constitutes a body of darkness, crudely empty, and could stand for the agonic state of absolute dispossession. In a note to a picture in the series that forms *Still Water*, Horn asks, 'What is the darkness in the Thames?' In a subsequent note, she responds, 'The Thames is you.'[140] This question and its answer are repeated throughout Balka's oeuvre. *How It Is* is a dry Thames.

13. Open graves
Balka grew up in Otwock, Poland, and learnt about power through a familiarity with the history of invasions, massacres and destruction in his country. He embraced the historical responsibility *vis-à-vis* the Nazi *différend* (he was born in 1958), opposed State terrorism and the repressive nature of the Communist regime and reacted against the censorship imposed by a Catholic education. There is a tendency to think that darkness devours light. From his experience Balka knows

that the opposite is true: white marble is fed by the darkness of political opacity. It is worth referring here to Conrad's description of Brussels as the 'whited sepulchre',[141] a metaphor that refers to Belgian colonial violence in Africa under King Leopold II. Here, Conrad echoes the New Testament: 'Woe to you, scribes and Pharisees, you hypocrites. You are like whitewashed tombs, which appear beautiful on the outside, but inside are full of dead men's bones and every kind of filth'[142]

Balka's grandfather was a monumental stonemason and made tombs at the cemetery in Otwock from terrazzo (chips of polished marble). Operating in this symbolic place of existential loss since 1944, his father still works as a carver and engraver of names and dates on tombstones. He is a craftsman of memory. In this 'symbolic chain', instead of becoming the third generation to sculpt only with solid materials, Balka chose the more dynamic, symbolic materiality of smell, sound and film. He sculpts with the signifiers of life and death, construction and loss: soap, human hairs (which like cut flowers, are actually cadavers), pine needles (leaves lost to the tree), and live maggots. Walls made of ash or displays of drawings burned in a studio fire show the artist's eschatological effort to overcome destruction by establishing an ultimate destiny for lived materials.

Martin Herbert argues that Balka's 'ludic set of funerary, transubstantiated equivalences depended on Balka's mobilising of what Brian O'Doherty once called "the sacramental nature of the space".[143] Masaccio's fresco *Saint Peter Healing the Sick with his Shadows* in the Brancacci Chapel in Florence, shows Saint Peter walking though the lame and blind; they are cured as his shadow falls on them. *How It Is* can promise neither healing nor vision. The 'blind' signifier of *How It Is* menaces ocularcentrism by stimulating imagination to heighten nyctophobia. Balka articulates a *coincidentia oppositorum* (coincidence of opposites) in pursuing presence in absence, and exploring the conceptual clarity of darkness through its symbolic density. He takes darkness to illuminate our cognitive visual effort and political consciousness. The open grave stands for the visitor who must abandon the role of passively understanding linguistic expression and take up the task of reactivating meanings.

14. Barbarian darkness and the architecture of the camps

'Before World War II, seventy-five per cent of the population were Jews', says Balka of his childhood town. 'I grew up in a house that was two streets away form the border of the ghetto. The soil was full of pain. For so many years I lived without knowing the real history.'[144] Eight thousand Jews from Otwock were taken to Treblinka in 1942 as part of the Nazi Final Solution. In his notes for *How It Is*, Balka wrote 'some Treblinka Stangl?' (referring to Franz Stangl, the SS Obersturmführer of Treblinka), and crossed this out. But the words 'Babi Yar' also appear on the list. Thus Balka encompasses two levels

of moral debasement around the Holocaust: the Shoah itself, and the omission of acknowledgement connected to it. This is a starting point for unravelling his cartography of evil: Majdanek, Treblinka, Auschwitz – described by Hannah Arendt as empirical 'laboratories where the fundamental conviction of totalitarianism that everything is possible is verified'[145] – and Babi Yar, which for Balka stand for execution without trial.

Babi Yar is a ravine in Kiev (Ukraine). In 1941, an estimated 33,771 Jews were killed in a single massacre by Sonderkommande 4. The Jews were herded to the bottom of the ravine to be shot. The site became the largest collective tomb of the Shoah.[146] *How*

Balka's father engraving a tombstone for the exhibition *+GO–GO (1985–2001)*

It Is becomes a vicarious memorial for the *yar*, described in Yevgeny Yevtushenko's poem *Babi Yar* as the 'soundless scream'. Darkness is Balka's mode of sculpting the depths of the ravine of uncertainty in the history of the Holocaust. He works with lightless vision to make a primal step into that uncertainty, which motivates him to draw, with dramatic containment, an association with an earthly hell.

'On one day at the end of the twentieth century I asked myself what I do for the ones who lived here and are gone', recalls Balka. 'And I started my pilgrimages to the concentration and death camps ... To collect their traces and take care. First Majdanek near Lublin. I was there as a child with a school excursion. Nobody mentioned any Jews killed there.' His examination of the history of Majdanek resulted in works like *The Walk* 2001 and *Bon Voyage* 2004, based on footage of the camp.

Balka's cartography in these works is neither physical geography, nor a mapping of darkness. The sculptor explores the unstable territory of the *homo sacer* and takes his place as a wanderer between places of extermination. The *homo sacer* is an individual who lives a vulnerable existence as an exile. The *corpus* of Balka's sculptures might have more in common with Art Spiegelman's graphic novel *Maus: A Survivor's Tale* (1986) than with much contemporary sculpture. *Maus*, in which the Jews in the concentration camps are depicted as mice, tells of the struggle of Vladek

Spiegelman, the author's father, to survive in a Nazi camp. Maus is the *homo sacer*, a body, as Giorgio Agamben described it, that 'in its capacity to be killed but not sacrificed, [is] a living pledge to his subjection to the power of death.'[147]

In the work *536 x 434 x 5 + The Walk* 2001, Balka retraced the last steps of the prisoners in the forced labour camp of Majdanek. A video projected onto the floor records his view of the bathhouse floor, as he walks slowly, following the journey of the vulnerable *homo sacer* in the camp. The vertiginous images reinforce the instability of the political ground depicted. 'I am a part time archivist using my video camera', says the artist. For the second element, Balka built a replica of the camp's bathhouse, (which lay next to its gas chamber) and filled the gaps between the planks with salt. Salt is the material reduction of bodily sweat and tears, which are representative here of the physical effort of forced labour (referencing the phrase *Arbeit macht frei* – 'Work Brings Freedom' – on the gates of Auschwitz) and emotional energy (the painful utterance: 'how could this happen?').

How It Is addresses its critical versatility both to the hidden spaces of the extermination camps and to exhibitionist Nazi architecture. To the question 'What is German Art?' Adolf Hitler responded that 'To be German means to be clear', a model which, according to Barbara Miller Lane, later came to apply to German art, architecture and the Nazi State

Miroslaw Balka
536 x 434 x 5 + The Walk
2001
Wood, salt and video

itself.[148] Architecture, whether traditional or modern, according to the official ideology and propaganda should be heroic and grand. Hitler himself commissioned the modern and neoclassical buildings of the House of German Art in Munich, designed by Paul Ludwig Troos in 1933, and the Zeppelinfeld in Nuremberg, a monumental grandstand developed in 1934–8 by Albert Speer and inspired by the Pergamon altar. The bland box of *How It Is* is comparable to Speer's reductive cubic mass, which hosted Nazi ceremonies of up to 200,000 people. In 2008, Tate Modern had a total of 5,236,702 visitors, or over 400,000 per month. Balka's inverted parody of Nazi grandeur derives from the placement of *How It Is* at the bottom of the Turbine Hall ramp. This vantage point is opposed to the grand perspectives of Nazi architecture. In addition, Balka thrusts the pervasive Nazi signifier of 'clarity' into opacity.

Die Rampe was both the title of the catalogue for Balka's shows in Eindhoven and Lodz in 1994 and the working title for his *690 x 190 x 102* 2006. Beyond that Turbine Hall ramp and the larger body of *How It Is* there is another ramp that takes the viewer into the sculpture. This has resonance for Balka with the Treblinka experience, who explains that in Poland the phrase 'being on the ramp' meant that one was embarking for the Treblinka camp. In fact, it is actually the lack of architecture in Treblinka that interests Balka: 'Strange place. No barracks, no watch towers like in the other places. Almost empty. Erased place.'[149] Even though *How It Is* is not a piece of architecture, it nevertheless deals with those traces just as much as more overtly referential works such as *250 x 700 x 455, Ø 41 x 41/Zoo/T*, a skeletal structure based on the octagonal building that housed a menagerie of animals to amuse the guards at Treblinka. Balka rescaled the height of this zoo to 250cm, which was the maximum height he could reach above his head. Form comes together with a sense of his own body, of what is graspable by the artist, a sense of limit.

The efficiency of Treblinka, 'that machine perfectly au point', allowed it to receive large numbers of inmates, and to exterminate them with just two hour's notice.[150] The name of Stangl on Balka's list confirms his focus on the architectural structure of extermination. 'My conscience is clear', Stangl declared at his trial. 'I was simply doing my duty.' He was found guilty of around 900,000 deaths. Unlike the camp death machine, *How It Is* in this context is no longer to be interpreted as a devouring machine, but a device for knowledge against denial and oblivion. With spatial economy, Balka proposes a process of transference to the viewer of the critical responsibility of constructing an awareness of the truth. *How It Is* responds to Balka's imperative of consciousness regarding the negative agenda of the Holocaust and confronts itself with the unthinkable, the unutterable, the ungraspable or the irreducible to images. The frightening surprise might be finding the nothingness there and yet still having to challenge these

Miroslaw Balka
250 x 700 x 455,
Ø 41 x 41/Zoo/T
2007/8
Steel, electric light, red wine and pump

limits. Darkness is associated here with deprivation of any support or hope – in the camp, and in the museum.

Balka started to map the Holocaust in 1993 with a work related to Auschwitz, *A Crossroads in A*. However, the nature of the materials, form, agenda, and social inscription of these works are not to be seen as either imagined architecture or maquettes of camp pavilions. His *170 x 126 x 10 / T.Turn* 2004, a video projection onto a bed of salt, describes the 360-degree movement of Balka's camera, which is strapped to his hands as he rotates his body on the ground near the ramp in Treblinka (p.91). The blind image is a destabilizing vertiginous landscape. Later, in *Primitive* 2008, Balka reduced to a three-second loop footage taken from Claude Lanzmann's nine hour film *Shoah* (1985). Lanzmann interviewed survivors, witnesses, and perpetrators from the camps of Treblinka and Auschwitz-Birkenau. Balka's film featured just two words, uttered by former Treblinka SS guard Franz Suchomel –'zwar primitive' – Treblinka was primitive, he said. The architect

Daniel Liebskind has also engaged with issues of the spatial articulation of the Holocaust. With the Jewish Museum in Berlin (1999), he uses spatiality to offer visitors a drastic experience as an approach to the suffering under the Shoah. The radical drama of light and darkness achieved by Liebskind creates a feeling of entrapment, disorientation and annihilating loneliness. Balka, too, aims to create situations of engagement through bodily experience and the phenomenological perception of places. Both build monuments to the final experience through fractional instants rather than making great gestures of resistance. In this sense, *How It Is* belongs to a family of works by Christian Boltanski, Anselm Kiefer, Art Spiegelman, Guillermo Kuitca, Vera Frenkel, and many others. Saul Friedlander contends that the Holocaust cannot be recounted through language, literature, art, or philosophy – that it lies beyond the limit of representation. By contrast, Barbie Zelizer defends a 'multivalent jump' with which to leap 'into the terrain that utilizes the visual as the simultaneous high and low ground of the Holocaust representation, a default setting for considering the Holocaust not only through high modes of visual representation but also through recent phenomena such as virtual reality or tattoos … Each domain needs to be considered on its own terms.'[151] It is necessary to examine how Balka's references to the Holocaust sit in relation to these views. Art has made crucial shifts in the process of breaking the silence around the Shoah. Boltanski,

for instance, has focused on the resistance of memory against erasure. Primo Levi has disinterred the entire history of the Reich in a war against forgetting.[152] Similarly, Balka's intention is to break the silence of his lived experience in Otwock.

Kiefer's generation worked within a framework of German guilt, shame and distress regarding the Second World War and the Holocaust. In *The High Priestess / Zweistromland* 1985–9, two bookcases containing hundreds of books on a vast superhuman scale map the zone of the three Abrahamic religions. Charles Molesworth has discussed whether Kiefer's adoption of a German tradition of architectural grandiosity is a betrayal of the Holocaust, as some critics have asserted. In opposition to Friedlander, he argues that 'Kiefer – especially if read through several critical viewpoints at once – is actually using *both* an ironic and didactic mode.'[153] Balka, like Kiefer, has insufflated aspects of Judaism, Christianism and Islamism in *How It Is*, but unlike Kiefer, the metonymic Balka has chosen his own human scale to guide the symbolic dimensions of his art. Balka does not seek grandeur and redemption. This brings him close to the sometimes unredeeming philosophy of Hannah Arendt regarding the collapse of civilization, oblivion, the failure of intellectuals, and the lack of responsibility assumed by the perpetrators. The art of Balka explores whether democracy is attainable through the kind of self-analysis advocated by Adorno. Balka refutes positivism and resists any idea of

Miroslaw Balka
*Stills from 170 x 126
x 10 / T.Turn*
2004
Steel, salt, video

mimetic truth in the work. Thus he refuses any form of human figuration. His choice is the presentation of places or of actual human physical indexes like hair.

'I was in Auschwitz in 1992, but did not understand too much,' Balka recalled. In his list of references, the acronym 'DH' appears, standing for (Georges) Didi-Huberman, 'whose *Images malgré tout* I read at that time'. Only four photographs are extant from Auschwitz, hence the annotation '4 images from A' in the list. Taken in 1944 by Aleks, an unidentified Greek Jew, they are the sole images of extermination, including crematorium activities and execution. In *Images malgré tout* Didi-Huberman asserts that these photographs do not simply provide evidence of the horror of the Nazi regime, but were deliberate acts of political resistance to make the world aware of the scale of annihilation in the fully operating Auschwitz-Birkenau camp. Didi-Huberman calls them 'four pieces of pellicle scratched from hell'.[154] Shot against all odds, they do not exorcise or sublimate. The camp was the blindest of all spots. There is neither pathos in the photos of Aleks nor in the place created by Balka at Tate Modern.

Finding *Images malgré tout* was instrumental for the constitution of an ethos in Balka's approach to the Holocaust. 'To know something you must be able to picture it yourself', is the initial sentence of this book. *How It Is* is a complex place for that experience. Didi-Huberman is in disagreement with Lanzmann on the way to approach ethics. The former maintains that photographs should enunciate, speak out of their silence, whilst for Lanzmann the sole possibility is enticing viewers to listen, see and think. Artists undergo similar concerns with regards to the issue of presence in their work. Balka goes beyond a tragic epiphany or an aesthetic sensuous experience. He confronts viewers with an alternative present reality that conveys a sense of diagramatic presence of what can be perceived. Zygmunt Bauman has asserted that the 'Holocaust was born and executed in our modern rational society, at a high stage of our civilization and at the peak of human cultural achievement, and for this reason it is a problem of that society, civilization and culture.'[155] Balka's sculpture articulates Bauman's and Adorno's assertion that art should keep the symbolism of the Holocaust alive, as well as Arendt's argument that the totalitarian regimes of Nazism and Socialism were fundamental fractures in history, corroding moral, political and philosophical categories like the Enlightenment. Perhaps for Balka an answer can begin to be found in the words of Paul Celan: 'Only one thing remained reachable, close and secure amid all losses: language. Yes, language. In spite of everything, it remained secure against loss. But it had to go through its own lack of answers, through terrifying silence, through the thousand darknesses of murderous speech.'[156]

15. *Plague of Darkness*

The Biblical plague descended as the Hebrews of Egypt were freeing themselves from bondage: 'And the Lord said unto Moses, Stretch out thine hand toward heaven, that there may be darkness over the land of Egypt, even darkness which may be felt'.[157] *How It Is* takes that notion to discuss vision from the perspective of darkness. At the foundation of monotheism, frogs, gnats, wild animals, epidemics, skin boils, hail, locusts, not seeing and death are God's negotiation language of choice for the Hebrews. Balka invokes blindness, plagues and wanderings when he makes reference to Gustave Doré's illustration of the *Plague of Darkness* (c.1866) for the Bible.[158] Nonetheless, *How It Is* surpasses the idea of a minimalist reduction of the plague to a geometric solid. The artist convokes the plague as the presence of the intangible, the tactile and the impossibility of seeing.

Cildo Meireles's *Blind Mirror* 1970 (p.56) consists of a rectangular 'canvas' covered with a malleable mass to be moulded by visitors, similar to the tactility of Braille. Meireles confirms vision through touch, like the tactile gaze of the blind man of Puiseaux described by Diderot: 'A mirror is a machine,' he says, 'which puts things in relief, far from themselves ... It is like my hand, it is enough to put it on an object to feel it.'[159] The flock interior that the visitor to *How It Is* encounters in the darkness similarly relies on a way of seeing that rests beyond the visible.

When discussing Balka's *a,e,i,o,u* (p.94), Rottenberg stated that vowels are so self-explanatory they do not merit graphic representation in some languages: 'Consonants are the true instruments of articulation; a secondary form of communication – full of complexity, misunderstanding and lies.'[160] Lying and praying share a linguistic common ground in Balka's oeuvre. Thus, Noah's Ark, the Eucharist, or the Ka'ba are connected to *How It Is*. According to medical literature, the nyctophobic reaction to Balka's piece for the Turbine Hall would include breathlessness, lack of control, heightened senses and panic attacks. For Balka, neither darkness nor art poses a threat commensurate with the fear of it. He dislocates the phenomenology of perception to another bodily experience. Where vision fails, any talk, any sound, makes it lighter for Freud's nyctophobic child, Diderot's blind man, the person who prays, or the viewer at Tate.

Rottenberg's mention of 'misunderstanding and lies' raises Balka's concern with the linguistics of lying. Just as praying, art criticism or the scotophobic symptoms of the visitor are dealt with in *How It Is,* so too is lying.[161] This comparison of lying with religion allows for the problematicisation of darkness. Derrida asks, 'Can we pray without understanding the language?' Balka is stating that sometimes art is not to be understood either. 'One can pray without knowing the words,' hopes a spiritual Derrida.[162] Can we be appeased by any oral rumor whether a truth or a lie? Are lies told with

Gustave Doré
'The Ninth Plague of
Darkness' from The
Doré Bible, engraved
by Pannemaker,
published by Gassell
Petter & Galpin,
London, Paris and
New York 1870
Engraving

words only? *How It Is* restores
darkness from being a ruined word.
Its lexical meaning aspires to create
corollaries of textual meaning in
mythology, philosophy, Marxism,
psychoanalysis and so on. To resist
lying, for *How It Is* Balka has
developed narrow, precise, individual,
and concrete textual meanings:
Auschwitz, Africa, black holes, desire,
the unconscious, shells. The idea of
darkness as a dangerous place,
following the reasoning of Harald
Weinrich's *The Linguistics of Lying*,
verifies that words or material signs
do not sit alone. If this were not so,
How It Is could involuntarily fall into

the same dangerous rhetoric
categories of euphemism, hyperbole,
ellipses, amphibole, formulas of
politeness, emphasis, irony, verbal
taboos, anthropomorphisms and the
like that force our thoughts into lies.[163]
When Rottenberg mentions lying as
an issue for Balka, she actually
reinforces the differences between
the corollaries of lexical meaning and
textual meaning in the articulation of
language. Understanding the semiotic
traps, she contrasts lying with 'the
truth of language.'[164]

In the *différend*, the truth of language
is at stake. Balka confronts the

différend, a difference between reason and imagination. Lying may be inside the *différend*, as it was with the Nazi Final Solution. Lyotard has talked about a situation where one 'is divested of the means to argue and becomes for that reason a victim,' where differences are neutralised and the result is a silence due to the difficulty of expressing an injustice, almost as if there were no consequences.[165] *How It Is* asserts that darkness confronts the impossibility of fully enunciating the dimension of an injustice, personal or collective, and yet implies a willingness to acknowledge it.

16. Bakka

Miroslaw Balka has assembled three spiritual dimensions of the Islamic tradition to discuss *How It Is*: Mecca, Ka'ba and the pilgrimage. As a linguistic inflexion, the name of the artist will appear in this paragraph with the accents of his native Polish. The *Sacred Qu'ran* tells us that 'The first House [of worship] / appointed for men was that of Bakka: full of Blessing / and of guidance / for all kinds of beings'.[166] Bakka is an older name for Mecca. Thus, Bałka is an imperfect anagram for Bakka, presently Mecca.[167] The anagrammatic difference derives from the diacritical letter from the Polish alphabet and its sound, which is more like an English 'l' than a graphically similar k. The interconnecting references of *How It Is* allow for such linguistic games.

Earlier, there was discussion of how the virtual depth of *How It Is* goes far beyond the limits of 3,900 cubic metres, in the same way that 1,800 cubic metres cannot account for the immense spirituality of the Ka'ba. In the *Qu'ran*, the 'Unbelievers' state is similarly vast: 'the depths of darkness in a vast deep ocean, overwhelmed with billow topped by billow, topped by [dark] clouds depths of darkness, one above another'.[168] Balka surpasses the antagonism between the self and the visual experience of darkness as mediated by social frameworks such as faith or the museum. He affirms that darkness 'is never black black',[169] thus resonating with Wittgenstein's remark that 'dark and blackish are not the same concept.'[170]

Balka touches on discussions about Western and Islamic positions towards knowledge and truth. In the twelfth century, the Islamic philosopher Ibn Rushd (Averroës) wrote *The Incoherence of the Incoherence*,[171] in which he attacked the argument that Aristotelianism is irreconcilable with Islam and defended the Aristotelian theory of truth. Balka can be seen to align himself with Averroës in this way. Balka's oeuvre is opposed to a neo-Platonic metaphysics of light for he

Muslim pilgrims pray in the holy city of Mecca, Saudi Arabia

embraces no uninstantiated properties of darkness. Thus dissimilar forms of incommensurability, like the Ka'ba and *How It Is*, reiterate the impossibility of comparing value differences.

The pilgrimage to Bakka entails the ritual circumambulation (*Tawáf*) of the Ka'ba. *How It Is* does not follow this sacred geometric path. Balka troubles the relationship between the abstract idea of religion and contemporary aesthetics, art and capitalism. We are no longer in the museum as 'spiritual beings' or a pilgrim in the Ka'ba pavilion with its black *Hajar-ul-Aswad*. In late capitalism, pilgrimage has been substituted by tourism. Guy Debord understood that 'tourism, human circulation considered as consumption, a by-product of the circulation of commodities, is fundamentally nothing more that the leisure of going to see what has become banal'.[172] A 'glimpse of *ersatz* eternity' is to be found in the artistic circuit of the white cube, the shrine of art in advanced capitalism.[173] The visitor to *How It Is* is a perambulator, a destinerrant stroller in darkness, and cannot be compared with the circumambulator pilgrim to Mecca with their devotional intentionality. Balka has established a place with no route or arrival point. In a parody of O'Doherty's *Inside the White Cube*, Balka's institutional critique turns off the light in the tool box of critics, curators and collectors. The 'white cube' became the umbrageous region for an unheard pilgrimage. The layered information surrounding the signifier of *How It Is* assures that the only possible rational expectation is never reaching any final conclusion. *How It Is* is a *locus* for being in a state of doubt as an epistemological experience.

17. Malevich: black on darkness.
Balka is constantly reshaping that assertion made by Merleau-Ponty that language is not only 'born', 'but also developed in obscurity'.[174] He sculpts the need to utter. In his installation *a,e,i,o,u*, shown in the context of the discussions about anthropophagy at the twenty-fourth Bienal de São Paulo (1998), two openings in a wall led to a sealed space in darkness to which the only communicative access was the sound of barking dogs. The work is organised within a symbolic economy that rests on an enticing suspicion of communication. According to Anda Rottenberg, *a,e,i,o,u* indicated power and the symbolic impotence of vestigial forms, 'a dialectics of the desired and the undesired',[175] which bears comparison with the anthropophagic and the anthropoemic aspects of *How It Is*. 'Enclosure, darkness and lack of non-emotional communication transform the process of reasoning into empathy', argues Rottenberg. The perimeter of the internal architecture of *How It Is* displaces the non-verbal frontier of *a,e,i,o,u* even further towards a political dimension to his pheno-menology of darkness and towards association with a Suprematist lack of objects. Linda Boersma observes that 'though Suprematist paintings might lack objects, they are not without form and content.'[176]

In *Manifesto of the Non-object* (1960), the poet and art critic Ferreira Gullar

Miroslaw Balka
a,e,i,o,u
1997
Plywood, leather,
steel, audio

takes the work and theories of Malevich and Mondrian as a starting point to discuss Lygia Clark's *Bichos* 1960, Hélio Oiticica's *Nucleous* 1960 and Lygia Pape's *Book of Creation* 1959 –60. 'The non-object is not an anti-object, but rather a special object in which the synthesis of sensorial and mental experiences are expected to be realised; it is a body transparent to phenomenological knowledge, integrally perceptible, which is given to perception without leaving any trace. A pure appearance.' *How It Is*, like mirrors, leaves no trace. In the same way as the non-object demands active participation (no longer making a mere spectator of the visitor), *How It Is* is a construct to be completed by the viewer.

'One thing was clear to Goethe', said Ludwig Wittgenstein – and this is also understood by Balka – 'no lightness can come out of darkness – just as more and more shadows do not produce light.'[177] In this sense Wittgenstein is a *pre*-Malevich thinker. In his conceptual discussions, the scale of luminosity includes extreme light, grades of shadow and extreme darkness. In the same way, a 'sliding scale' of lexical meanings of the word 'darkness' occurs in the context of *How It Is*. Balka does not wish to simply play the Wittgensteinian language-game of reporting on the greater lightness or darkness of bodies.[178] For him, darkness is not the collapse of the *language* of the visible, but a confrontation with the radical *visual* concept of darkness. For Balka it is not merely a matter of discussing the nothingness, but rather of substantiating darkness in emptiness as an equating of space with political density. *How It Is* does not merely offer the void. Malevich stresses that in Suprematism, 'the condition of being a surface plane does not exist, the square is only one of the facets of the Suprematist prism through which the world of phenomena refracts itself'.[179]

Rottenberg has suggested that Balka's *a,e,i,o,u* might be recited like a *zaum* verse. *Zaum*, a language that relies on sound symbolism, was created by Aleksei Khruchenykh with the poet Velimir Khlebnikov for the libretto of Futurist opera *Victory over the Sun* 1913. The music was composed by Mikhail Matyushin and Malevich designed the stage set. The alogic of *zaum* left its mark upon Malevich. Korneï Tchoukovski described *zaum* as the language of the word in itself, which finds in itself its own end.[180] Along the same lines, Malevich reaffirmed his consciousness of the principle of 'art as an end in itself'.[181]

For Malevich the mirror is zero. 'If art has achieved knowledge of harmony, rhythm, beauty, it has achieved knowledge of zero…The essence of diversities. The world as non-figuration', he writes in *The Suprematist Mirror*.[182] In anticipation of Suprematism, the backdrop designed by Malevich for *Victory Over the Sun* displayed a black square. On the eve of the First World War, the sun in the opera was taken to refer to the decadent past, buried by the Strong Men of the Future. The sun, one more Symbolist theme to be scorned, is reshaped at the dawn of Cubo-Futurism. At the end of the opera, an airplane crashes and a curtain bearing the image of the sun is torn apart. El Lissitzky saw this as a celebration of the technological capacity of man: 'the sun as the expression of the world's age-old energy is torn down from the sky by modern man; the power of his technical supremacy creates for itself a new source of energy.'[183] For Malevich, the sun is a black Suprematist square. He thinks of cognition through colour to attain the 'free white abyss'.[184] Similarly, Balka would work with neither the symbolisation, figuration nor representation of the sun, and yet, the visitor to this lightless place dwells in the sun: Balka's strategy with his list and its additions, substitutions, subtractions, is to inflict on *How It Is* 'a plague of light', an excess of possible meanings that maintains its unfixed symbolic state.

18. '… the whole things coming out of the dark'
There is nothing there, except darkness. *How It Is* substantiates nothingness in the visual unconscious and ennunciates the experience of a state of semantic agnosia. An actively mute discourse, *How It Is* is an anti-iconic operation. Darkness imposes the impossibility of narrative. Daniel Birnbaum has observed that Samuel Beckett is the 'quintessential interrogator of the coherent self and liberator of the voice'.[185] Like Adorno, Balka has learnt that Beckett's works are absurd not because of the lack or absence of meaning, but because they put meaning on trial.[186]

How It Is is an imageless place. Art history enters a state of eclipse. The sculptor proposes an experience similar to that described by Hans-Georg Gadamer: 'one feels the attraction of a precise meaning while also being aware that this meaning is withheld, perhaps even deliberately concealed.'[187] Under this condition, the Thing – *das Ding* – remains undomesticated. Loquacity finds a state of asymbolism derived from the excess of layers of references. The vowels of Balka's *a,e,i,o,u* can in this way stand for *a*-artistic, *e*xtermination, *i*nnumerate, *o*bfuscation and the *u*nutterable.

The non-existent horizon inside *How It Is* gives the eye the experience of looking 'to the faraway plafond where it can see no one', as described by Beckett.[188] It has been necessary to overwhelm the sculpture with rhetorical references in order to produce its exhaustion. Balka takes the dark emptiness of *How It Is* as a confrontation between the audience and the desert of visual language that connects with Beckett's project in literature: 'The expression that there is nothing to express, nothing with which to express, nothing from which to express, no power to express, no desire to express, together with the obligation to express.'[189]

Beckett can be seen to represent in literature what Arnold Schoenberg represented in music for Theodor Adorno in his *Aesthetic Theory*. From the 1940s, the philosopher aimed to grasp the meaning of culture post-Auschwitz. This is a matter that Balka

Miroslaw Balka
Cain
1987
Wood, carpet, textile, steel, paint

considers socially unresolved. Adorno departs from his understanding of the ground zero of Beckett's literature, to see it as unfolding forces in infinitesimal physics: 'a second world of images springs forth both sad and rich, the concentrated historical experiences that otherwise, in their immediacy, fail to articulate the essential: the evisceration of subject and reality.' Adorno moves on to draw abstract conclusions about art: 'Art carries out the eclipse of concretion, an eclipse to which expression is refused by a reality in which the concrete continues to exist only as a mask of the abstract.'[190] In this sense Balka's work attends to some of the problems enunciated in art by Adorno via Beckett. If Beckett's ground zero is the 'warmth of the primeval mud impenetrable dark', the grave simplicity of Balka's sculpture, which takes the past as a political necessity to build the critical density of the present, finds its own ground zero. His viewers take their first step from that moment.

In *Waiting for Godot*, Beckett leaves us in doubt as to whether a certain point in the day is sunset or dawn, though Vladimir asserts that 'night is drawing nigh'.[191] This state of doubt about place and time is inscribed in Balka's sculpture. In using the same structure to discuss the metaphors of both Plato's cave and the extermination camp, he projects knowledge and obscurantism into the same space. The artist takes from Beckett the drive to extinguish the images by which we define ourselves. Balka's Beckettian operation pursues the luminous darkness, after depleting the image through the exploration of a rich repertoire of references. He exhausts images and what lies beneath them.[192] Exhaustion, singularity and lack of definition are the Beckettian qualities of *How It Is* that deliberately confound, frustrate and exhaust the audience.

Bruce Nauman has revealed that the presence of certain movements in his work is due to the influence of Beckett's stories: 'for example, Molloy transferring stones from pocket to pocket … They're all human activities; no matter how limited, strange, and pointless, they're worthy of being examined carefully.'[193] Many other artists have acknowledged their legacy to the writer: Sol Le Witt,

Joan Jonas, Mona Hatoum, Stan Douglas, and Ana Miguel amongst them. The Beckettian issue at work among the Minimalists, and in the art of Nauman and Balka, is lack of communication – which they resolve in the dissolution of metaphysicality.

In his 1964 book *How It Is*, from which Balka takes the name of his work, Beckett writes 'on my face in the mud and the dark I see me it's a halt nothing more I'm journeying it's a rest nothing more.'[194] The challenge for this artist is in establishing a field of impenetrable darkness that reaches beyond the *semantics* of darkness. 'As the audience understands that there is neither the sublime nor beauty to be found … if there has to be any

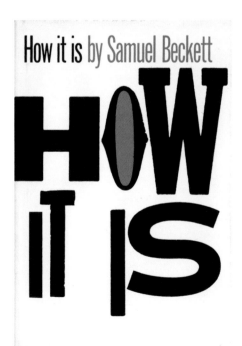

How It Is by Samuel Beckett, cover art by Roy Kuhlman. Grove Press, New York, 1964.

feeling, perhaps the feeling would be disillusion. Beckett wishes for "an art unresentful of its insuperable indigence and too proud for the farce of giving and receiving"'.[195] Many works by Balka, such as *How It Is* and *Oasis (C.D.F.)* 1989 (p.109) are taken to the verge of falling within this 'insuperable' form of 'indigence' due to the extreme simplicity of their materials and their precarious structure. The work is insistently irreducible to narrative.

Mud is the primeval impenetrable dark of Beckett's *How It Is*.[196] For *Endgame*, all Beckett demanded was an empty room and two windows.[197] Balka adopts this same perverse paring down for the Tate work: an economy of nothingness that might disrupt the expectations of the visitor to the white cube.[198] In his case, he does not even allow Minimalist precision and elegance to take over the discourse, avoiding the labelling of his work. Balka could be seen to be inviting the viewer of *How It Is* to visit Beckett's *How It Is* and the 'ill-said, ill-heard, ill-recaptured, ill-murmured in the mud'.[199] The final question to be put to the sculptor might be one asked by Slavoj Žižek in discussing the sublime object of ideology: 'Why is there something instead of nothing?'[200] *How It Is* consists of a ramp, a large steel box and darkness.

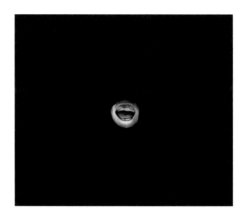

Billie Whitelaw as the mouth in Samuel Beckett's *Not I* at the Royal Court Theatre, London, 1973

Endnotes:
[1] Jack the Ripper, Kain, Spaceship Apollo, JMC, BG, and Big black vibrator are some of the references that will not be commented on in this text.
[2] Joseph Conrad, *Heart of Darkness*, in *Heart of Darkness and Selected Short Fiction*, ed. George Stade, New York 2003, p.123.

[3] Ernst Cassirer, *An Essay on Man*, New Haven 1944, p.26.
[4] Jean François Lyotard, 'Preface: Reading Dossier', in *The Differend: Phrases in Dispute*, trans. Georges Van Den Abbeel, Minneapolis, 1988, p.xiv.
[5] Miroslaw Balka in an email to the author, 31 July, 2009.
[6] Guy Debord, *Society of the Spectacle*, Detroit 1983, unpag., §165.
[7] Roland Barthes, *The Rustle of Language*, trans. Richard Howard, Berkeley 1989.
[8] Ferdinand de Saussure, *Cours de linguistique générale* (1916), Paris 2005, p.108.
[9] Jacques Derrida, *Writing and Difference*, trans. Alan Bass, Chicago 1992, p.27.
[10] See Roland Barthes, *Mythologies*, Paris 1957, p.193.
[11] The Islamic astronomer, mathematician and philosopher Abu Ali al-Husain ibn Abdallah ibn Sina (965 – c.1039), known as Avicenna, compared the eye to a mirror, The eye, through this understanding of visual perception gained the Latin term *speculum animarum*.
[12] 'Light brings the mirror to life' according to Oliver Leaman in *Averroës and his Philosophy*, London and New York 1997, p.94.
[13] Plato, *Republic: Books 6–10*, trans. Paul Shorey, Cambridge 2006, p.423.
[14] 'Plato on poetry and painting', in *The British Journal of Aesthetics* 1982 vol.22, no.2, p.126–37.
[15] For other issues of Plato and Hades, see Cristina Ionescu, *Plato's Meno: An Interpretation*, Lanham 2007.
[16] Jacques Lacan, *Some Reflections on the Ego*, Apud Dylan Evans, *An Introductory Dictionary of Lacanian Psychoanalysis*, London 1996, p.115.
[17] In *Écrits*, trans. Bruce Fink, New York 2002, p.75.

18 Jacques Lacan, *O Seminário, Livro 4: a relação de objeto,* ed. Jacques-Alain Miller, trans. Dulce Duque Estrada, Rio de Janeiro 1995, p.15.

19 The resulting conflicts and agressions can be dispensed with in the present discussion.

20 Fink 2002, p.77.

21 Jacques Lacan, *Seminar, Book 10: L'angoisse,* apud Evans 1996, p.116.

22 In this sense, *How It Is* converses with Cildo Meireles's *Blind Mirror* 1970 a tactile mirror where the glass is substituted with a soft synthetic wax, which spells out the title of the work in Braille. The blind can thus sense this image on the surface of the object without substantial loss of meaning.

23 David Summers, *Vision, Reflection, and Desire in Western Painting,* Chapel Hill NC 2007, p.21. The author is indebted to Summers for the historical data about painting in Greece in this chapter.

24 Summers 2007, p.26.

25 Roland Barthes, *The Responsibility of Forms: Critical Essays on Music, Art, and Representation,* Berkeley CA 1991, pp.212–13.

26 Plato, *The Republic: Books 6–10,* trans. Paul Shorey, Cambridge MA 2006, Book VII, 514a–520a

27 Ibid., pp.177–9.

28 Ibid., p.179.

29 Ibid., p.174.

30 The author is indebted to Paul Virilio here.

31 In *Human, All Too Human,* Hollingdale, Cambridge 1996, vol.II, p.344.

32 Miroslaw Balka, as dictated for an email from Helen Sainsbury to the author on 18 June 2009.

33 'On the soul', in *The Complete Works of Aristotle,* ed. Jonathan Barnes, trans. J.A. Smith, Princeton 1991, vol.1, book II, 1, p.2.

34 See G.B. Kenfeld, 'Pneuma', in Paul Edwards (editor in chief), *The Encyclopedia of Philosophy,* New York 1967, vols.5 and 6, p.361.

35 *Da natureza afetiva da forma na obra de arte* (1949), in Otília Arantes (org.), 'Mário Pedrosa: Forma e Percepção estética', São Paulo 1995, p.107.

36 Genesis 6:15.

37 Genesis 7:2.

38 Dante Alighieri, *The Divine Comedy,* vol.1, *Inferno,* trans. Robert M. Durling, New York and Oxford 1996, *Inferno,* Canto 1:2.

39 Apud John Forrester, '"Mille e tre": Freud and Collecting', in John Elsner and Roger Cardinal (eds.), *The Culture of Collecting,* Cambridge 1994, p.227.

40 In an email to the author dated 13 July, 2009.

41 Saint, Teresa of Avila, *Autobiography,* Chapter XXIX, part 17, trans. David Lewis, London and New York: 1904 [EBook #8120; 2005].

42 In an email to the author dated July 13, 2009.

43 *The Language of Psycho-analysis,* trans. Donald Nicholson-Smith, New York 1973, p.431.

44 Karl Marx and Friedrich Engels, *The German Ideology,* ed. C.J. Arthur, trans. W. Lough, New York 1970, p.47.

45 Ibid., p.147.

46 See Alain Badiou about Malevitch, *Le Siècle,* Paris 2005, p.86.

47 Fredric Jameson, '"End of Art" or "End of History"?' in *The Cultural Turn,* London 1998.

48 Louis Althusser, *Aparelhos ideológicos de Estado,* trans. Walter João Evangelista and Maria Laura Viveiros de Castro, Rio de Janeiro 1992, p.68.

49 Lyotard 1988, p.12.

50 Karl Marx, *Capital,* trans. Ben Fowkes, London 1990, vol.I, p.1050.

51 See Slavoj Žižek, *The Sublime Object of Ideology,* London 2008, p.15.

52 Ibid., p.16.

53 Gilles Deleuze and Félix Guattari, *Anti-Oedipus: Capitalism and Schizophrenia,* trans. Robert Hurley, Mark Seem and Helen R. Lane, Minneapolis 1998, pp.35 and 38.

54 Cildo Meireles, 'Zero cruzeiro/Zero centavo', in *Cildo Meireles,* Rio de Janeiro 1981, p.30.

55 Fredric Jameson, 'Transformations of the Image in Postmodernity', in Jameson 1998, p.135.

56 *Caminhando* is an experience of immanent time exemplified by the act of making a longitudinal endless cut in paper to form a Moebius band.

57 See Jürgen Habermas, 'The Entwinement of Myth and Enlightenment: Max Horkheimer and Theodor Adorno', *The Philosophical Discourse of Modernity,* trans. Frederick G. Lawrence, Cambridge 1992, p.119.

58 In the translation by Ronald L. Martinez and Robert M. Durling: 'rays of the planet that leads us straight on every path' (*raggi del pianeta che mena dritto altrui per ogne calle*' (*Inferno,* Canto 1: 17–18, pp.26–7).

59 '*là dove il sole tace*'

60 Mary Lynn Johnson and John E. Grant (eds.), *Blake's Poetry and Designs,* New York 1979, p.119.

61 In the Brazilian translation by Joaquim Paiva, *Ensaios sobre a fotografia,* Rio de Janeiro 1981, p.3.

62 *Camera Lucida: Reflections on Photography,* trans. Richard Howard, New York 1981, p.80.

63 The scholarly work of Philip Steadman analyses how Vermeer explored the science of optics, applying the camera obscura to his canvases: Philip Steadman, *Vermeer's Camera: Uncovering the Truth behind the Masterpieces,* Oxford 2001.

64 Johnson and Grant 1979, p.96.

65 Vilém Flusser, *Towards a Philosophy of Photography,* trans. Anthony Matthews, London 2000, p.21.

66 Ibid. p.27.

67 See Steadman 2001, p.24.

68 Brian O'Doherty, *Inside the White Cube: The Ideology of the Gallery Space*, Berkeley CA, 1999, p.41.

69 Ibid., p.15.

70 Ibid., p.14.

71 'The Darkness Inside a Stone', in Henry Meyric Hughes et al., *Anish Kapoor*, London 1990, p.13.

72 *A Poética do espaço*, trans. Antonio da Costa Leal and Lídia do Valle Santos Leal, Rio de Janeiro, undated, pp.138–56.

73 All quotes were taken from the English version translated in 1934 by Abdullah Yúsuf 'Alí. *The Holy Qu'ran*. Elmhurst 2005. Commentaries n.48 to the *Súra Bagárah* 2:12, p.51.

74 In Gregory Battcock (ed.), *Minimal Art: A Critical Anthology*, New York 1968, p.92–102.

75 Ibid.

76 Gottlob Frege, *The Foundations of Arithmetic: A Logico-mathematical Enquiry into the Concept of Number*, trans. J.L. Austin, Evanston IL 1992, p.115.

77 Ibid., § 87, p.99.

78 'Box of 1914', in *Salt Seller: The Writings of Marcel Duchamp (Marchand du Sel)*, ed. Michel Sanouillet and Elmer Peterson, New York 1973, p.22.

79 Frege 1992, § 27.

80 These correspond to notions and issues of number discussed by John Allen Paulos, *Innumeracy: Mathematical Illiteracy and its Consequences*, New York 2001, pp.3–18.

81 See Roland Omnès, *Quantum Philosophy: Understanding and Interpreting Contemporary Science*, Princeton 1999, p.19.

82 'The Origins of Geometry', in Jacques Derrida, *Edmund Husserl's Origins of Geometry: An Introduction,* trans. John P. Leavey, Jr., Lincoln NE 1989, pp.158–9.

83 Interview with the author on 14 January, 1999.

84 Jean-Pierre Luminet, *Le destin de l'univers*, Paris, 2006, Chapters 14 ('Le trou noir machine') and 15 ('Le trou noir quantique'), pp.322–55, was an important basis for discussions in this chapter.

85 Luminet articulates mathematician Claude Shannon's theory of information and the so-called entropy of Ludwig Boltzmann, in ibid., p.324.

86 Apud Thomas McEvilley, 'La peinture monochrome...', in *La couleur seule*, Lyon 1988, pp.15–16, in this French version: *sans dessus-dessous et écartelé*.

87 In Ronald Duncan and Miranda Weston-Smith (eds.), *The Encyclopaedia of Ignorance* (Oxford 1977), D. Gough, B. Bertotti, and P.D. Wall wrote on these three subjects respectively. More than thirty years have elapsed since the publication of this title, therefore major scientific advancements have occurred in most fields covered by the book.

88 Gaston Bachelard, *La Poétique de l'espace* (1957), Paris 2008, p.62. It has been translated into English as *The Poetics of Space*.

89 See *The Lure of the Local: The Sense of Place in a Multicentered Society*, New York 1998.

90 Tzvetan Todorov, *Les abus de la mémoire*, Paris 1995, p.9.

91 Miroslaw Balka, Interview with Jaromir Jedlinski, in *Die Rampe*, exh. cat., Van Abbemuseum, Eindhoven 1994, p.69.

92 Miroslaw Balka, Interview with Jaromir Jedlinski, in ibid p.64.

93 *A Poética do espaço*, trans. Antonio da Costa Leal and Lídia do Valle Santos Leal, Rio de Janeiro: undated, pp.138–56.

94 For the relationship between Dickinson and Bachelard see Maria Lúcia Milléo Martins, '"Intimate immensity" in Emily Dickinson', *Fragmentos*, no.34, January – June 2008, pp.91–8.

95 Bachelard, *A Poética do espaço* (undated), p.109.

96 Sigmund Freud, *A General Introduction to Psychoanalysis* (*Vorlesungen zur Einführung in die Psychoanalyse*) rev. ed. by Joan Riviere, 1924, Preface by Ernest Jones and G. Stanley Hall, New York 1953, p.414.

97 In an email to the author dated 8 July, 2009.

98 The Greek word *nyx*, has contributed to form other medical terms, such as 'nyctalopia' (night blindness) and 'nyctanopia' (vision impairment in darkness and dim light).

99 Barthes 1989.

100 Bachelard, *A Poética do espaço*, p.95.

101 Miroslaw Balka, Interview with Jaromir Jedlinski 1994, p.64.

102 Miroslaw Balka, Interview with Jaromir Jedlinski 1994, pp.69–70.

103 See Gilles Deleuze, *A Dobra: Leibniz e o Barroco*, trans. Luiz B.L. Orlandi, Campinas 1991; and Robert Merrihew Adams, *Leibniz: Determinist, Theist, Idealist*, Oxford 1998.

104 Deleuze 1991, p.17. Translation by the author.

105 *The Ethics of Psychoanalysis*, *Seminar* VII, ed. Jacques-Alain Miller, trans. Dennis Porter, London and New York 1992, p.121.

106 Miroslaw Balka in an email to the author, 31 July, 2009, All quotations from Balka in this chapter were taken from this message.

107 'The Caves of Gallizio and Hirschhorn: Excavations of the Present', *October*, Spring 2006, no.116, pp.87–100.

108 See by the author, 'Le Corbusier', in *Louise Bourgeois*, exh. cat., Tate Modern, London 2007, pp.89–90.

109 Adolf Max Vogt, *Le Corbusier: The Noble Savage*, Cambridge MA 2000, p.201 and 211.

110 Translation by the author.

111 Jack Lindsay, *Gustave Courbet: His Life and Art*,

London 1977, p.217.

[112] George Hersey, *The Monumental Impulse*, Cambridge 2001, p.117.

[113] Ibid., p.135.

[114] Ibid., p.138.

[115] 'Ornament and Crime' ('*Ornament und Verbrechen*') (1908), in Ulrich Conrads, *Programs and Manifestoes on 20th Century Architecture*, Cambridge 1975, pp.19–24.

[116] Deleuze and Guattari 1998, p.3.

[117] Lucretius, *The De Rerum Natura of Titus Lucretius Carus,* trans. Rolfe Humphries, Bloomington IN 2008, Book V (158–202), p.165.

[118] *Lucretius on Creation and Evolution: A Commentary on De Rerum Natura, Book Five, Lines 772-1104,* Oxford 2003, p.45.

[119] J. Laplanche and J.B. Pontalis, 'Source of the Instinct', in *The Language of Psychoanalysis,* trans. Donald Nicholson-Smith, New York 1979, v.424. The authors call attention to the diversity of meanings that the term 'source' has in Freud's theory.

[120] Slavoj Žižek*, The Fragile Absolute,* London 2000, p.33.

[121] See Dylan Evans, *An Introductory Dictionary of Lacanian Psychoanalysis,* London and New York 2005, p.82.

[122] Jacques Lacan, *Seminário 11: Os quatro conceitos fundamentais da psicanálise*, org. Jacques-Alain Miller, trans. M.D. Magno, Rio de Janeiro 1990, p.95.

[123] Harald Szeemann, '"Zeitlos" – "Intemporel"', *Écrire les expositions,* Brussels 1996, p.127.

[124] Claude Lévi-Strauss, *Tristes Trópicos,* trans. Wilson Martins, São Paulo 1957, pp.414–15.

[125] See Michael Cronin, *Translation and Globalization,* London and New York 2003, p.95.

[126] Jeremias Bentham, *El Panoptico,* trans. Julia Vera and Fernando Alvarez-Uría, Madrid 1989, p.36.

[127] Ibid., p.30.

[128] *The Art of Art History*, Oxford 1998, p.507.

[129] Martin Herbert, 'Miroslaw Balka', *Frieze*, no.71, November – December 2002, p.106.

[130] *Rabelais and His World,* trans. Hélène Iswolsky. Bloomington 1984, p.145 ff.

[131] Ibid, pp.141–2.

[132] *Songs of Innocence*, in Mary Linn Johnson and John E. Grant (ed.), *Blake's Poetry and Designs*, New York 1979, p.22.

[133] Frantz Fanon *The Wretched of the Earth*, trans. Constance Farrington, New York 1966, p.126.

[134] *Roni Horn: Still Water*, exh. cat., SITE Santa Fe, 2000, Note 18 of Plate 6, Pages not numbered.

[135] Joseph Conrad, *Heart of Darkness*, in *Heart of Darkness and Selected Short Fiction*, George Stade (ed.), New York 2003, pp.42–3.

[136] Dante Alighieri, *The Divine Comedy*, ed. and trans. Robert M. Durling, New York and Oxford 1966, vol.1 *Inferno*, pp.47.

[137] Exh. cat., Sante Fe 2000, Note 29 of Plate 8, Pages not numbered.

[138] *Home and Exile*, Oxford 2000, p.79.

[139] Olu Oguibe, *The Culture Game*, Minneapolis 2004, p.11.

[140] Exh. cat., Santa Fe 2000, Note 15 of Plate 18, Pages not numbered.

[141] Conrad 2003, p.44.

[142] Martin Herbert, 'Miroslaw Balka', *Frieze*, no.71, November – December 2002, p.106.

[143] Matthew 23:27.

[144] Miroslaw Balka in an email to the author, 31 July, 2009.

[145] 'Les Origines du totalitarisme', *Les Origines du totalitarisme, Eichmann à Jerusalém*, ed. Pierre Bourtez, trans. Jean-Loup Bourget, Robert Devreu and Patrick Lévy, Paris 2006, p.182.

[146] References to Babi Yar were drawn from Richards Rhodes, *Mestres da Morte: a invenção do Holocausto pela SS nazista*, [*Masters of Death: The SS Einsatzgruppen and the invention of the Holocaust*] trans. Mauro Gama, Rio de Janeiro, 2003, 187–96.

[147] Giorgio Agamben, *Homo Sacer: Sovereign Power and Bare Life,* trans. Daniel Heller-Roazen, Stanford CA 1998, p.99.

[148] 'Arquitectura Nazi', In Xavier Sust et al., *La arquitetura como símbolo del poder*, trans. Emma Bragulat de Martín, Barcelona 1975, pp.78–9.

[149] Miroslaw Balka in an email to the author, 31 July, 2009.

[150] Jean-François Steiner, *Treblinka: la revolte d'un camp d'extermination*, Paris 1966, p.266.

[151] Barbie Zelizer (ed.), 'Introduction on visualing the Holocaust', in *Visual Culture and the Holocaust*, New Brunswick 2000, p.2.

[152] Primo Levi, *Les naufragés et les rescapés*, Paris 1989, p.31.

[153] 'The Art of Memory: Anselm Kiefer and the Holocaust', in Alan Milchman and Alan Rosenberg, *Postmodernism and the Holocaust*, Amsterdam 1998.

[154] *Images malgré tout*, Paris 2003, p.11.

[155] Zygmunt Bauman, *Modernity and the Holocaust*, Ithaca 1989.

[156] 'Speech on the Occasion of Receiving the Literature Prize of the Free Hanseatic City of Bremen.' in Paul Celan, *Collected Prose*, trans. Rosmarie Waldrop, Riverdale-on-Hudson 1986, p.34.

[157] Exodus 10:21–3.

[158] From *La Sainte Bible: Traduction nouvelle selon la Vulgate par Mm. J.-J. Bourasse et P. Janvier*, Tours 1866.

159 Denis Diderot. *Lettre sur les aveugles à l'usage de ceux qui voient* (1749), Paris 2000, p.31.

160 Anda Rottenberg, Paulo Herkenhoff and Adriano Pedrosa, *XXIV Bienal de São Paulo: Representações nacionais*, exh. cat., Fundação Bienal de São Paulo, Sao Paulo 1998, p.224. Rottenberg is the main scholar on the work of Miroslaw Balka, and has been following his work since 1985.

161 Scotophobia, lygophobia and achluophobia are synonyms of nyctophobia.

162 Jacques Derrida in conversation with Michael Govrin and David Shapiro. *Body of Prayer: The Heavens that Shall be Folded Together as a Book.* ed. Kim Shkapich, New York 2001, p.59.

163 Harald Weinrich, *The Linguistics of Lying and other Essays*, trans. Jane K. Brown and Marhal Brown, Seattle 2005, p.12.

164 Ibid., p.28.

165 Jean-François Lyotard, *The Differend: Phrases in Dispute*, trans. Georges Van Den Abbeele. Minneapolis 1992, p.13.

166 *The Holy Qu'ran*, Súra Ál-i-'Imrán 3:96.

167 Ibid. 24:40

168 The imperfect anagram Bałka / Bakka is possible through the using the English translation of the *Holy Qu'ran* named here and cannot be applied to all translations.

169 In an email to the author dated 8 July 2009.

170 Wittgenstein 1978, III: 104, p.29e.

171 'L'incohérence de l'Incohérence', *Averroès. L'Islam et la raison*, trans. Marc Geoffroy, Paris 2000, pp.161–204.

172 Guy Debord, *Society of the Spectacle*. Detroit 1983, unpag., § 168.

173 See Thomas McEvilley. 'Introduction', in O'Doherty 1999, pp.9 and 10.

174 *Phénoménologie de la perception*, Paris 1987, p.449.

175 Anda Rottenberg, 'Complementary Empathy', in exh. cat., Sao Paulo 1998, p.224.

176 Linda S. Boersma, *0,10 The Last Futurist Exhibition of Painting*, Rotterdam 1994, p.48.

177 Ludwig Wittgenstein, *Remarks on Colour*, ed. G.E.M. Anscombe, trans. Linda L. McAlister and Margarete Schättle, Berkeley CA 1978, III: 126, p.33e.

178 Ibid., p.34e.

179 Kasimir Malevich, 'La lumière et la couleur', In *La lumière et la couleur* (1923–6), trans. Jean-Claude Marcadé and Sylviane Siger, Lausanne 1993, p.71.

180 K. Tchoukovski, 'La langue Zaum', in *Les futuristes* (1922), trans. Gérard Conio, Lausanne 1976, pp.49–50.

181 Kasimir Malevich, 'Le tract 0-10', in *Le miroir suprématiste*, trans. Jean-Claude and Valentine Marcadé, Lausanne 1977, p.153.

182 Kasimir Malevich, 'Le miroir suprématiste', in Malevich 1977, p.97.

183 'The plastic form of the electro-mechanical peepshow "Victory of the sun"' (1923), in Sophie Lissitzky-Küppers (ed.), *El Lissitsky*, trans. Helen Aldwinckle, London 1992, p.352.

184 Kasimir Malevich, 'Le suprematisme' (1919), In Malevich 1977, pp.83–4.

185 Daniel Birnbaum, *Chronology*, New York 2005, p.21.

186 Theodor W. Adorno, *Aesthetic Theory*, trans. Robert Hullor-Kentor, Minneapolis 1997, p.153.

187 Hans-Georg Gadamer, *Gadamer on Celan: 'Who Am I and Who Are You?' and Other Essays.*, trans. Richard Heinemann and Bruce Krajewski, New York 1997, p.167.

188 Samuel Beckett, *Le dépeupleur*, Paris 1970, p.7.

189 'Three Dialogues with Georges Duthuit', in Samuel Beckett: *Disjecta: Miscellaneous Writing and a Dramatic Fragment*, ed. Ruby Cohn, London 1983, p.139.

190 Adorno 1997, p.31.

191 'Waiting for Godot', in Richard W. Seaver (ed.), *I can't go on, I'll go on – A Samuel Beckett Reader*, New York 1991, p.465. Unless otherwise mentioned, all quotes from Beckett were taken from Seaver's anthology.

192 This sentence paraphrases Brian Evenson on his review of the writings of Deleuze about Beckett, especially on the latter's *Film*, at time of writing this is posted on the site http://mail.architexturez.net/+/ Deleuze-Guattari-L/archive/msg21896.shtml.

193 Coosje van Bruggen, *Bruce Nauman,* New York 1988, p.18.

194 *How It Is*, Beckett/Seaver 1991, p.509.

195 'Three dialogues', Beckett/Cohn 1983, p.140.

196 Garin Dowd, *Abstract Machines: Samuel Beckett and Philosophy after Deleuze and Guattari*, Amsterdam and New York 2007, p.170.

197 Selma Klein Essink refers to Beckett's *Endgame* in the article 'Mankind the Measure of all Things', in *Die Rampe*, exh. cat., Van Abbemusum, Eindhoven and Museum Sztuki, Lodz 1994, p.41.

198 The expression 'economy of nothingness' was coined by Steven Connors in relation to Beckett, apud Garin Dowd 2007, p.209.

199 *How It Is*, Beckett/Seaver 1991, p.509.

200 Slavoj Žižek, *The Sublime Object of Ideology,* London 2008, p.77.

Film still showing a
volcano in Ethiopia
from *Le Feu de la
Terre*, directed by
Polish-born French
director, vulcanologist
and geologist Haroun
Tazieff
1994

Roni Horn
from *Still Water
(The River Thames,
for Example)*
1999
Off-set lithograph
printed on white
wove paper

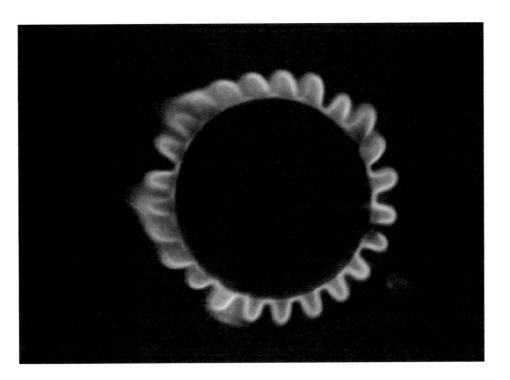

Miroslaw Balka
2 x (170 x 126 x 10) / BlueGasEyes
(detail)
2004
Steel, salt, video

Simulation of a black hole, a hypothetical region of space in which the gravitational pull is so powerful that nothing, not even light, can escape

A Bitter Happiness[1]

Helen
Sainsbury

*The past: something real, but absolutely
beyond our reach, towards which we
cannot take one step, towards which
we can but turn ourselves so that an
emanation from it may come to us.
Thus it is the most perfect image of
eternal, supernatural reality.*

*Is it for this reason that there are joy
and beauty in remembrance as such?*
−Simone Weil[2]

It is late October 2008 and night has
just fallen on Miroslaw Balka's home-
town of Otwock, twenty-eight
kilometres outside of Warsaw. Visiting
the artist for the first time I have taken
in the atmosphere of the house in
which he grew up, which now serves
as a studio. In the failing light, Balka
has shown me the rooms that have
stood as silent witnesses to so much
of his life and work. Sculptures and
drawings, new and old, partial and
complete, line the walls or nestle on
shelves and in boxes. The remains
of another work, a heap of rock salt
mined from Klodawa Salt Mine,
central Poland, occupy one corner,
standing as a makeshift monument
to the sweat and tears of miners and
their families.

Later, we visit the cemetery which
houses the tombstones and monuments
sculpted by his grandfather, a
stonemason, and engraved by his
father. In Britain the gates would have
been locked at dusk, all lights long
extinguished. In Poland, the gates
stand open and the cemetery is
illuminated by hundreds of candles
lit in memory of those who will shortly
be celebrated on All Souls' Day.
Returning to Warsaw, the city's vast
monuments reinforce the vitality of the
Polish people's respect for history but
it is the more intimate memorials of
Otwock that cast the longest shadow.

It is undeniable that Balka has spent
much of his career turning to face the
past, his work holding a mirror to
Weil's 'perfect, eternal reality'. Yet
Balka's is not an art of nostalgia. The
horrors of twentieth century history
are met, if not exactly head on, then
with a respect for accuracy and detail,
inevitably rendering this interface
deeply uncomfortable. Yet somewhere
among the harsh facts of history there
lies an area of uncertainty, which
might best be characterised as a
certain tenderness, a respect for
humanity, that pervades his work.

Balka's early performances and
sculpture referred to his experience of
a strict Catholic upbringing, perhaps
made more intense in a country
where, under Soviet rule, religion was
repressed. In recent years he has
focused on the Holocaust, which for
Balka rightly exists as a permanent
scar on collective memory, with
particular resonance in the towns
where he has lived: Otwock and
Warsaw. Despite the austerity of form

and seriousness of his subject matter, Balka's work is often imbued with warmth and humour, perhaps reflecting his view that 'After seeing the sadness inscribed in the works maybe some spectators can see that joy can also be found in those moments of life that one lives to the full'.[3]

In his early work, Balka explored the human experience through figurative sculptures of the body, sometimes combined with performance art. However, in the late 1980s, his work became more abstract. The human figure appeared to be absent, yet its presence was nevertheless strongly implied, not least by the dimensions of the work, which often correspond to Balka's own height or the extent of his reach. Visiting the graveyard in Otwock highlighted the close parallel between these seemingly abstract works and the monuments made by his grandfather – after all, what is a grave if not a manifestation of the corporeal limits of the human body? Paradoxically, as Balka has focused ever closer on Polish history, he has begun to work on an increasingly large scale. In recent years there has

been a subtle shift towards a mode in which the participation of the viewer has become more prevalent; structures have become more monumental, albeit still anchored to the size of his own body in some way. 'Kissing the hand of history', as he has called it, is apparently important to Balka on a personal, communal and universal level.[4]

Given the close correlation between the size of the human body and the dimensions of his sculptures, Balka may seem an unlikely choice for a commission in such a vast space as Tate Modern's Turbine Hall. Always envisioned as a great social space and closer to a covered street than the normal entrance hall of an art gallery, it acts as a decompression chamber between the bustle of the outside world and the rarified atmosphere of the art museum. As the Unilever Series of commissions has unfolded over the years, it has also highlighted the special relationship that has grown up between the public and the art that has occupied this space. Watching visitors interact with the crack inserted into the floor of the

Turbine Hall by Doris Salcedo in 2007, Balka was struck by the fact that the artist could not control the way the public reacted to the work. Despite the severe ideological schisms addressed by Salcedo's work, there were as many viewers enjoying the 'spectacle' of the piece and behaving with levity and humour as those who surveyed the work thoughtfully. As the gallery gradually filled up each day, a strange kind of choreography would take place as visitors lined the edges of the chasm. However, of all the works that have occupied the Turbine Hall, it was Olafur Eliasson's *Weather Project* that really captured the imagination of the public. Every day thousands would flock to the building to spend time sitting, walking or lying in the space, contemplating Eliasson's gleaming sun and regarding their own reflections in the mirrored ceiling. The hall became a social space, a spiritual destination and even a political arena when visitors spelled out words with their bodies to protest against the visit of George W. Bush.

Perhaps it is inevitable that the public should react in this way. One need not look too far to find examples of humankind's innate desire to connect and play intervening in even the most adversarial of situations – the much-cited Christmas football match between British and German troops during the First World War, for example. Yet it seems that for most people tragedy seems more potent than comedy. As Balka has put it, for most of us, 'being united in happiness is less important than being united in pain'.[5] However, he has also

commented that however serious life may be, humour always somehow intervenes. It might also be said that there is often a redemptive quality to be discovered within his work. *Ding,* a film by Balka, illustrates this point effectively. Whilst making the film, Balka recorded a series of plates being thrown against a wall and smashing. The cycle of destruction was broken when one plate bounced off the wall with a resounding 'ding' and landed intact. This is the moment that Balka's film portrays; this plate represents the one that got away, a glimmer of hope that should not be disregarded.

In *How It Is* Balka seeks to embrace the interactive traditions of the Turbine Hall. In keeping with much of his practice, his first instinct is to frustrate the viewer as they enter the space, being met first and foremost with a formidable wall of steel rising some fifteen metres above the lower floor and eight above the level of the bridge that spans it. Visitors will be able to walk underneath the work or along the two ravine-like spaces along the sides and only then will they be able to experience the full impact by entering the steel chamber. Ascending a steep slope upwards, the viewer will be confronted with a yawning cave-like space, the inky blackness of the interior contrasting sharply with the day-lit areas of the Turbine Hall. Balka's sculpture presents a bizarre twist on the surrounding architecture. Visitors are met with an inversion of the space – having descended the concrete ramp into the brightly lit Turbine Hall they will ascend a ramp into a pitch-black cavern. The solidity

Miroslaw Balka
The artist's studio
with elements of
Oasis (C.D.F.)
1989
Wood, steel, tin plate,
pine needles, plaster,
pump, milk, water

of the concrete and brick will contrast with the flexibility of the steel structure, in which each step will reverberate and echo around the interior, which encloses some 3,600 cubic metres of velvety darkness. Another shock awaits the visitor – the interior walls of the chamber are clad with a dense, black, flocked surface that sharply contrasts with the industrial steel exterior. For some, the flock will have either a luxurious or a homely feel, reminiscent of the grand wall-coverings of a stately home or the familiarity of the local curry house. For others, the flock will have an unnerving, almost animal feel, as if the interior of the chamber is clad with skin on which the hairs are standing on end. Likewise,

for some viewers stepping into the darkness will be a disorientating or frightening experience, whilst others will be enticed by the sense of mystery and adventure. Each will have to find their own limit, the point at which they decide to stop, or to put their trust into this darkness and forge ahead, cross this threshold.

Much has been written, in this catalogue and elsewhere, about the absence of light (or that almost palpable blackness) and its relation to the dark side of human nature. Yet Zygmunt Bauman here suggests that the darkness faced by the viewer may be rendered benign by the comfort of strangers sharing the experience.[6] In truth, it could go either way for any one of us. Balka's project thereby raises questions about the true locus of terror. Indeed, one might argue that the fears and unknowns represented by darkness are counteracted by the dangers of being out in the open, exposed. The dark dungeon of the past has been replaced by the starkly lit prison cell, whilst CCTV allows us to be under surveillance whenever we are in public. We may even be betrayed by the infra-red light emanating from our own bodies at night, leaving us almost nowhere to hide.

Balka's photographs of the perimeter fences of the dwellings in Lukasinskiego, the street in which he grew up, are another reminder of the vulnerable nature of being visible. Although the fences are high and therefore seem to be erected for the protection of the resident, they are all open railings or wire mesh and therefore transparent – there are no high walls or solid wooden fences as you might find in a British suburban street. Balka explains that during the Communist era walls were prohibited as they could be used to conceal activities that were not approved by the authorities. In our modern era, cameras track our every move and therefore privacy has become the ultimate luxury (p.112).

Liminal states
Taken from the Latin word *limen* (a threshold), the Oxford English Dictionary describes liminality as 'a transitional or indeterminate state between culturally defined stages of a person's life; *spec.* such a state occupied during a ritual or rite of

passage, characterised by a sense of solidarity between participants.' Balka's work was first shown at the Tate Gallery (now Tate Britain) in *Rites of Passage*, an exhibition of 1995 that captured important developments in contemporary art practice. A number of major works by the artist have subsequently been acquired for the Tate Collection, including *Dawn*, 1995, a multi-part sculpture which was first shown in the *Art Now* series at Tate Britain. In both instances, Balka addressed moments of transition – a rite of passage, as exemplified by his seminal work *Remembrance of the First Holy Communion* (p.27), or in *Dawn*, that brief passage of time that is neither night or day.

At the heart of many of Balka's works lies a confrontation, a moment at which one must negotiate a threshold, or perhaps a moment of looking in from the outside or out from the inside. Effectively, one is thrown into a liminal state, an instant in which anything might happen, as if one is teetering on the brink of something. It is perhaps also significant that where Balka's work touches most closely on the history of his country, it is often the means of transition, be it a ramp or path, which forms the backbone of the work. When we visited the extermination camp of Treblinka, around two hours drive from Warsaw, it became apparent that Balka was fascinated by the internees' means of arrival, such as the remains of the train track, as well as by the paths taken by the prisoners. He had researched the area thoroughly

enough to understand that the path now leading from the place where the prisoners were made to undress and the gas chambers was not the original path, known as *Schlauch* (tube) or *Himmelstrasse*, taken by the doomed prisoners.

I am reminded here of a significant episode in Andrei Tarkovsky's 1979 film *Stalker*. Perhaps one of the most extraordinary scenes in any film is a five minute sequence which shows the three main protagonists on a rail trolley, silently travelling towards their destination, a mysterious room that is rumoured to make the innermost wishes of its visitors come true. Ostensibly absolutely nothing happens, but it seems to me that this is where the three visitors become most truly themselves.

When Balka first suggested the title for *How It Is*, he used a sequence of gestures to amplify the meaning of his words. Drawing a circle with his hands he indicated that this described 'how'; holding his hands together in a firm but succinct downward movement he indicated the bare, ineluctable fact of 'it'; pushing his hands forward to indicate movement towards something symbolised 'is'. Balka's gestures may be seen as an abstraction of the movements of the visitors to his exhibition. The public will circulate around the structure (how), pause at the entrance to contemplate the darkness (it) and finally enter the chamber (is). Balka is thus inviting the viewer to step over that threshold, to enter the space and thus engage with whatever 'it' may be.

Traces

In *Fireplace* of 1986 (p.107), a pair of shoes sits at the edge of an old, worn carpet, the wearer apparently having re-entered the home for good and now seemingly fused with the building itself, both physically and symbolically, having literally become part of the fireplace. Obituaries from the local newspaper are papered over the simple brick hearth. These are replaced with new obituaries each time the work is shown, emphasising the constant cycle of life and death. A sense of melancholy pervades the drooping figure forming the hearth. It is as if the lives of those who once occupied this domestic space have impregnated the very fabric of the building.

An early example of Balka's more abstract works is *Oasis (C.D.F.)* 1989 (p.109), also in Tate's collection. Again, a domestic setting is evoked, but here the human presence is implied rather than depicted. A number of salvaged pieces of wood are combined to suggest a dwelling in which the daily rituals of human existence are played out. A wooden semi-circle represents the moon, suggesting a night scene. Two cradle-like containers hint at sleep whilst a coffin-shape affixed to the wall attached to a drainpipe, which appears to be circulating milk, again serves as a reminder of the eternal cycle of life. The reclaimed materials have a particular resonance for Balka. They include wooden planks from his childhood home and pine needles salvaged from a tree that grew up outside the window of the young artist. A simple piece of aged wood laid on the floor serves as a threshold, both inviting and denying the viewer entry into this domestic space. Dedicated to the German Romantic painter Caspar David Friedrich, Balka invokes both the spiritual and the everyday in this work.

In other works, bodily functions and fluids are hinted at by openings in the sculptures; labour and emotions are evoked by his use of salt (the residue of sweat or tears), and death by the use of ashes. Even for the new commission, which unlike many of Balka's sculptures will be built entirely from newly manufactured materials, the physical contact of visitors will eventually leave its legacy on the work – the moisture from people's hands will etch itself into the untreated steel exterior and the black interior will be abraded by the passage of those inside the chamber.

One source of inspiration for *How It Is* may be found in Balka's new studio. A small grubby steel box, acquired some twenty years ago from a rubbish dump, echoes the shape of the commissioned sculpture. Having lain in the garden for many years, its original purpose unknown by the artist, this simple box that opens at one end has now been identified as an early twentieth century surgical instrument – a sterilizer for surgical probes.[7] In many previous works, including *Dawn,* Balka has incorporated the use of soap into his sculptures, evoking the intimate yet universal rituals of cleansing whilst possibly offering some hope of

redemption. It therefore seems fitting that Balka should have been drawn to an object that has both contained and washed away the physical traces of human suffering.

What are you afraid of?
In 2000, when Balka's work was on show at the National Museum in Osaka, Japan, he was invited to run a workshop with local children. *What are you afraid of?* was his response to this task. For the first workshop, children coming to the museum were given drawing materials then asked to make a work on this subject. In a second workshop of 2005, *The Dark Side of the Day* (p.117), Balka wanted to see how they would respond to the challenge of making art about their anxieties with no illumination other than the light of a miner's lamp worn on their heads. The light emanating from the lamps was also partially obscured with marker pens to create an uneven spread of light as they worked. The children would therefore have the necessary comfort of areas of light by which to work, but the surrounding gloom and the sharply contrasting areas of shadow cast by the markings on the lamp created an arena in which the imagination could take flight. Like most children, monsters lurked in the dark corners of their imaginations, as well as spiders, and a fear of loneliness and being lost.

Balka has acknowledged that another major source of inspiration for *How It Is* comes from László Krasznahorkai's 1989 novel *The Melancholy of Resistance.* Set in a small town in

Fig. 272.

41. Sonde en argent, pour femme. . . .   **3** »
42. Sonde en argent, pour homme, à
    double courant. . . . .   **15** »
43. Sonde en argent à double courant,
    pour femme . . . .   **12** »
44. Filière du Dr Gourdet, donnant la
    division par 1/3 mill. et celle de
    Béniqué (fig. **272**). . . . . . .   **5** »

Cette filière permet le calibrage des différents instruments urinaires y compris ceux de forme ovale, par exemple, du bec d'un lithotriteur. Il suffit de prendre les deux diamètres de l'instrument : leur somme donne le numéro de la filière de Béniqué ; leur moyenne celui de la filière Charrière. Les numéros de la filière Charrière sont ceux indiqués sur la filière elle-même ; une deuxième graduation, non chiffrée, divise la première et donne les numéros de Béniqué.

45. Filière nickelée, divisée par 1/3 de millim. (fig. **273**). . . . .   **4** »

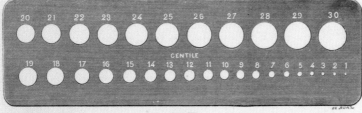

Fig. 273.

Stérilisation et Conservation des Sondes à l'état stérile

Fig. 274.

1. Stérilisateur au trioxyméthylène
    (formol), du Dr Janet, petit
    modèle, pour une vingtaine
    de sondes (fig. **274**). . . .   **35** »
2. Stérilisateur au trioxyméthylène
    (formol), du Dr Janet, grand
    modèle, pour deux cents son-
    des environ (fig. **275**). . . .   **150** »

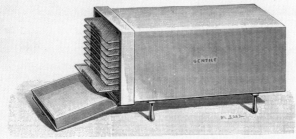

Fig. 275.

3. Stérilisateur au trioxyméthylène (formol), du Dr Janet, grand modèle, pour deux cents
    sondes environ (fig. **275**), mais avec porte vitrée . . . .   **160** »

From Collin Gentile,
Catalogue illustré d'Instruments de Chirurgie, 1905.

Hungary, it follows the events that ensue when a huge truck containing the body of a giant whale arrives in the main square. Visitors come to view this leviathan, but the true monster that arrives with the truck is a mysterious figure known as 'the Prince', whose incendiary words incite his followers to bring chaos and destruction to the society. We follow various characters as the events unfold: Mrs Plauf, who is afraid of anything that disrupts the status quo; Mrs Eszter, who seizes the opportunity of civil disorder to enhance her political power; and most poignantly, the innocent soul Valuska, who approaches the dark chamber wide-eyed with wonder:

Having managed to insert himself into the continually shuffling line, he finally reached the creature's jaws … but whether he stared down its dark throat, or tore his gaze away to survey its exterior to discover the two tiny eyes sunk in deep sockets on either side of the body … he was aware of seeing these things in isolation: it was simply impossible to see the enormous head as an integral whole.

It wasn't so much the mouth, nor the sheer incomprehensible size of the creature that most astonished him, but the full and certain general knowledge purveyed by the publicity that it had witnessed the wonder of an infinitely strange and infinitely distant world, that this gentle yet terrifying denizen of the great seas and oceans was actually here, and one could even take the liberty of touching it.[8]

Events in the novel take on a terrifying turn as riots break out all around. The protagonists are buffeted around the town by episodes of violence, while the whale lies at the eye of the storm, the only point of stillness and certainty. A comparison might here be made with Balka's great dark chamber, which will occupy the vast Turbine Hall, acting almost as a centre of gravity around which the visitors will circulate. Like Krasznahorkai's whale, its meaning will depend largely on the beholder and the encounters that they may have with others within.

How It Is might also be compared with the 'room' in *Stalker* described above. The eponymous protagonist acts as a guide for those seeking to enter the room, which may only be accessed by crossing 'the Zone' – an area of restricted land that is fraught with dangers. It is said that those who cross the threshold will be granted their innermost desire, yet the 'Stalker' and his two companions (a writer and a professor) choose not to enter. The writer's greatest fear is that he has not recognised his deepest wish and therefore may be horrified to discover the true nature of his desires. The professor has come with the intention of destroying the room for fear of what will happen if the 'wrong' people use the room for personal gain, but is ultimately dissuaded by the Stalker, who recognises that the true value of the room lies purely in the hope and faith that it represents. Somewhere in all three projects there lies an unknown. In *Stalker*, the cynical writer and terrified professor risk life and limb to reach the threshold yet turn away; in *The Melancholy of Resistance*, it is the innocent, Valuska, who marches boldly into the trailer containing the body of the whale, the tranquil eye of the storm around which social order disintegrates.

Which leaves us with *How It Is* and one remaining question – how will it be for each of us?

Endnotes:

[1] Inspired by a line from Andrei Tarkovsky's 1979 film *Stalker*: 'It's better to have a bitter happiness than a dull, grey life.'

[2] Simone Weil, *Gravity and Grace*, Reading 1987, p.155.

[3] Juan Vicente Aliaga, 'Danse Macabre: An interview with Miroslaw Balka', in *Revision 1986-1997*, exh. cat., Ivam Centre del Carme, Valencia 1997, p.144.

[4] 'Miroslaw Balka interviewed by Iwona Blazwick', in *Possible Worlds: Sculpture from Europe*, exh. cat., Institute of Contemporary Arts and Serpentine Gallery, London 1991, p.16.

[5] 'Danse Macabre: An interview with Miroslaw Balka', ibid., p.149.

[6] see pp.14–23.

[7] Collin Gentile, *Catalogue illustré d'Instruments de Chirurgie*, Catalogue No.1, Paris 1905, p.39.

[8] László Krasznahorkai, *The Melancholy of Resistance*, trans. George Szirtes, London 1999, pp.88–9.

Miroslaw Balka
The Dark Side of the Day
Educational workshop at the National Museum of Osaka, 30 July 2005

INTERIOR MERSEY TUNNEL, LIVERPOOL & BIRKENHEAD.
(UNDER THE RIVER MERSEY.)

G.270.   (73)

Postcard from a photograph taken inside the Mersey Tunnel, Liverpool

Postcard, written on back: 'The big German gun of Leugenboom at Moere. Interior view of one of the great ammunition shelters.'

A view of a blue whale skeleton in the Natural History Museum, London, 2007

Priest hole in the Kings Room at Moseley Old Hall, Wolverhampton

Hans Memling
The Last Judgement
(right-hand panel,
detail)
c.1469
Oil on panel

Chronology and Selected Bibliography

Biography

Miroslaw Balka was born in 1958 in Warsaw, Poland. In 1985 he graduated from the Academy of Fine Arts in Warsaw and from 1986 to 1989 worked together with Marek Kijewski and Miroslaw Filonik in the Consciousness 'Neue Bieriemiennost;'. In 1991 he received the Mies van der Rohe Stipend in Krefeld. He runs the Spatial Activities Studio at the Academy of Fine Arts in Poznan and lives and works in Otwock and Warsaw. His work is owned by museums worldwide including: Hirshhorn Museum, Washington DC; Moderna Galerija, Ljubljana; MOCA, Los Angeles; MOMA, New York; Museu Serralves, Porto; Muzeum Sztuki, Lodz; SFMOMA, San Francisco; Tate Modern, London; The Art Institute, Chicago; The Israel Museum, Jerusalem; National Museum of Art, Osaka; Van Abbemuseum, Eindhoven and Centre of Contemporary Art, Warsaw. He has also been commissioned to create a number of permanent outdoor works, including the memorial to the victims of the Estonia Ferry disaster in Stockholm (1997) and most recently at The University of California, Mission Bay, San Francisco.

Solo exhibitions

1985
Remembrance of the First Holy Communion, Zukow
Wolves-nowolves, TPSP, Warsaw

1986
Percepta Patris Mei Servivi Semper, Galeria Pokaz, Warsaw

1989
River, Galeria Labirynt 2, Lublin
Installation Abel, Galeria PO, Zielona Gora

1990
Good God, Galeria Dziekanka, Warsaw
xxx, Galerie Nordenhake, Stockholm

1991
xxx, De Appel Foundation, Amsterdam
April/My body cannot do everything I ask for, Galeria Foksal, Warsaw
IV/IX /My body cannot do everything I ask for,

Galerie Kacprzak, Cologne
XI/My body cannot do everything I ask for, Burnett Miller Gallery, Los Angeles

1992
No body, Galerie Peter Pakesch, Vienna
bitte, Museum Haus Lange, Krefeld
36,6, The Renaissance Society, Chicago

1993
36,6, MIT List Visual Arts Center, Cambridge MA
37,1, Galeria Foksal, Warsaw
37,1 (cont.), Polish Pavilion, 45th Venice Biennale
Die Rampe, Galerie Marc Jancou, Zurich

1994
Laadplatform + 7 werken, Van Abbemuseum, Eindhoven
Rampa, Muzeum Sztuki, Lodz
Buenas Noches, Galeria Juana de Aizpuru, Madrid
37,1, Lannan Foundation, Los Angeles
Rampen, Galerie Nordenhake, Stockholm
Winterhilfsverein, Moderna Galerija, Ljubljana

1995
J'ai en ma possesion, un certificat de vaccination contre le cholera, la fievre jaune, le typhus, la variole, Le Creux de L'Enfer, Thiers
Dawn, Tate Gallery, London
Un dia, Galeria Juana de Aizpuru, Seville
When you wet the bed (1987), Galeria Miejsce, Cieszyn

1996
Pause, Galeria Foksal, Warsaw

1997
Selection, Museet for Samtidskunst, Oslo
a,e,i,o,u, Galeria Foksal, Warsaw
Revision 1986–1997, IVAM, Valencia
a,e,i,o,u, Kunsthalle Bielefeld
Ordnung, Galerie Nordenhake, Stockholm
Out, London Projects, London

1998
Hygiene, Galeria Labirynt 2, Lublin

1999
sza, Galeria Foksal, Warsaw
manana, Galeria Juana de Aizpuru, Madrid
be good, Barbara Gladstone Gallery, New York

2000
Quit, White Cube, London
Between meals, National Museum of Art, Osaka

2001
*Around 21˚15'00"E 52˚06'17"N +GO–GO
(1985–2001)*, Galeria Zacheta, Warsaw
Pureza, Galeria Juana de Aizpuru, Seville
Ruhe, BWA, Zielona Góra
*Around 21˚15'00"E 52˚06'17"N +GO–GO
(1985–2001)*, SMAK, Gent
sweep, swept, swept, Barbara Gladstone Gallery,
New York
eclipse, Kroller-Muller Museum, Otterlo

2002
Nachtruhe, Galerie Nordenhake, Berlin
cekaonica, Museum of Contemporary Art, Zagreb
tiedtothetoe, Dundee Contemporary Arts, Dundee
dig,dug,dug, Douglas Hyde Gallery, Dublin

2003
Lebensraum, Fundacja Galerii Foksal, Warsaw
still, Anthony Meier Fine Arts, San Francisco
winterreise, Galeria Starmach, Krakow
Element die Exaktheit, Galleria Raffaella Cortese, Milan

2004
Karma, White Cube, London
Su Seguro Servidor, Galeria Juana de Aizpuru, Madrid
Neither, Gladstone Gallery, New York
Bon voyage, Musée d'Art Moderne at Contemporain,
Strasbourg

2005
kein warum, Galerie Nordenhake, Berlin
hipnoza, Galeria Arsenal, Bialystok

2006
kategorie, galeria ON, Poznan
du contrat social, Galeria Labirynt 2, Lublin
Lichtzwang, K21, Dusseldorf

2007
AAA + rauchsignale, Museum of Modern
and Contemporary Art, Rijeka
schmerzstillend, Galleria Raffaella Cortese, Milan
Cruzamento, Museo de Arte Moderna, Rio de Janeiro
Reflejos condicionados, Fundación Marcelino Botín,
Santander
Tristes Tropiques, Irish Museum of Modern Art, Dublin

2008
La salida, Galeria Juana de Aizpuru, Madrid
Entering Paradise + BGE, National Gallery
of Modern Art, Edinburgh

Landschaftsabfalle, Galerie Nordenhake, Berlin
Jetzt, WRO Art Center, Wroclaw
Nothere, White Cube, London
Crezyzewski, Galeria AT, Poznan

2009
Gravity, University of Massachusetts, Amherst
Und Akupunktur, Gladstone Gallery, New York

*Activity in the Consciousness 'Neue Bieriemiennost'
(a series of exhibitions and active vernissage done
in collaboration with Miroslaw Filonik and
Marek Kijewski)*

1986
One night flower, Pracownia Dziekanka, Warsaw
after Holiday presentation, Galeria Wieza, Warsaw
For Peace, Pracownia Dziekanka, Warsaw
For All Saints, Galeria Wielka, Poznan

1987
For Jean Bedel Bokassa, Galeria Stodola, Warsaw

1988
xxx, Galeria Rzezby, Warsaw

1989
Keine Neue Bieriemiennost, Galeria BWA, Bialystok

Group exhibitions
*denotes shows with accompanying
exhibition catalogues

1986
Expression of the 80s, Galeria BWA, Sopot *
Figures and Objects, Galeria BWA, Pulawy *

1987
2nd Biennale of the New Art, Zielona Góra *

1988
Sculpture in the Garden, SARP, Warsaw *
BKK (with M. Kruk and P. Kurka), HCAK,
The Hague *
Polish realities, Third Eye Centre, Glasgow *

1989
Middle Europe, Artist's Space, New York *
Dialog, Kunst Museum, Dusseldorf *
Feelings, Galeria Dziekanka, Warsaw

1990
Dialog, CSW, Warsaw *

1990
Aperto, 44th Venice Biennale *
Possible Worlds, ICA and Serpentine Gallery, London *

1991
Metropolis, Martin Gropius Bau, Berlin *
Kunst-Europe, Kunstverein Bonn *
Le mond critique, Kunstverein Hamburg *
Europe Unknown, Palace of Art, Krakow *
Borealis V, Kunstmuseum, Pori *
Korper und Korper, Kunstverein Graz
Rosa e Giallo, Galeria Pieroni, Rome *
Von Angesicht zu Angesicht, Stadt Galerie, Kiel *

1992
Documenta IX, Kassel *
The Boundary Rider, 9th Biennale of Sydney *
Polish avantgarde 1930–1990, Neuer Berliner
Kunstverein, Berlin *
Muzeum Sztuki w Lodzi–1931–1992 – Collection-
Documentation-Actualite, Musée d'art Contemporain
& ELAC, Lyon *

1993
Sonsbeek 93, Arnhem *
Rosa e Giallo, Le Cruex de l'Enfer, Thiers
De la Main a la Tete, L'objecte theorique, Domaine
de Kerguehennec *
Douce Ouvres Dans l'Espace, Domaine de
Kerguehennec *
Baltic Sculpture-Gotland 1993, Visby *
Artificial Paradises, Burnett Miller Gallery,
Los Angeles
Rosa e Giallo, La Criee, Rennes
Restaurant, Restaurant la Bocca, Paris *

1994
Till Brancusi, Konsthall, Malmo *
Europa-Europa, Kunst und Austellung Halle, Bonn *
Tuning up-2, Kunstmuseum, Wolfsburg *

1995
ARS 95, Nykytaiteen Museo, Helsinki *
Incidents, Casa de Parra, Santiago de Compostela
Where is Abel, thy Brother?, Galeria Zacheta,
Warsaw *
Rites of Passage, Tate Gallery, London *
Ripple Across the Water, Watari Museum, Tokyo *
The Carnegie International 1995, The Carnegie
Museum of Art, Pittsburgh *

1996
City Space, Copenhagen *
Distemper, Hirshhorn Museum, Washington DC *
Horizons, Sonje Museum of Contemporary Art,
Kyongju *

Betong (with Anish Kapoor and Antony Gormley),
Konsthall, Malmo *
Pax (with Alfredo Pirri), Studio Tucci Russo,
Torre Pellice

1997
Niemensland, Museum Haus Lange, Krefeld *
Art from Poland 1945–1996, Mucsarnok, Budapest *
Umedalen Sculptur 1997, Galleri Stefan Andersson,
Umea *

1998
Wounds, Moderna Museet, Stockholm *
Displacements (with Doris Salcedo and Rachel
Whiteread), Art Gallery of Ontario, Toronto *
Privacy (with Luc Tuymans), Fundação de Serralves,
Porto *
XXIV Bienal de Sao Paulo *
Art and Environment, National Museum of Art,
Osaka *
10: Intensita in Europa, Pecci Museo, Prato *

1999
Three Stanzas (with Robert Gober and Seamus
Heaney), ICA, Philadelphia *
Ars Aevi, Museum of Sarajevo *
Trace, 1st Liverpool Biennial, Tate Liverpool *
Lost Paradise (with Zhang Huan), Galeria Presenca,
Porto *
Uchwyt, Muzeum Sztuki, Lodz
Distant similarities, National Gallery, Prague *
Held & let go, California Collage of Arts and Crafts,
Oakland *
Fauna, Galeria Zacheta, Warsaw
Aspects-Positions, Museum Moderner Kunst,
Stiftung Ludwig, Vienna *

2000
L'autre moitie de l'Europe, Jeu de Paume, Paris *
Negotiators of Art, Centre of Contemporary Art:
Laznia, Gdansk *
Vanitas, Virginia Museum of Fine Arts, Richmond *
Between Cinema and the Hard Place, Tate Modern,
London
Ombra della Ragione, Galleria d'Arte Moderna,
Bologna *
The Oldest Possible Memory, Sammlung Hauser &
Wirth, St Gallen *
Time and moments, Galeria Stara, Galeria Labirynt
2, Lublin *
Absolut Ego, Musée des Arts Decoratifs, Palais du
Louvre, Paris *
Wanas 2000, Wanas *
00, Barbara Gladstone Gallery, New York *
The Vincent, Bonnefanten Museum, Maastricht *
Through Melancholia and Charm, Galerie

Nordenhake, Berlin
Amnesia, Neues Museum Weserburg, Bremen *
Still, Alexander and Bonin, New York
Beware of Exiting your Dreams. You may Find Yourself in Somebody Else's, Galeria Zacheta, Warsaw
Scena 2000, Center of Contemporary Art, Warsaw *

2001
In Between, The Art Institute of Chicago & Cultural Center, Chicago
Negotiators of Art, Bunkier Sztuki, Krakow *
Oblicza smierci, BWA, Katowice *
Lugares de la Memoria, EACC, Castellon *
Milano Europa 2000, PAC e La Triennale de Milano, Milan *
Postawy, BWA, Lublin
Absolut Secret, Espace Tajan, Paris *
Biurokracja / Bureaucracy, Galeria Foksal, Warsaw *
New to the Modern, Museum of Modern Art, New York

2002
Conversation? Collection of Van Abbemuseum, Eindhoven, Academy of Fine Arts, Athens *
The Unthought Known, White Cube 2, London *
Arte all'Arte, San Gimignano *

2003
Dekada, Center of Contemporary Art, Warsaw *
About we, Van Abbemuseum, Eindhoven *
Distopia and Heterotopia between meals, Museum of Art, Hachinohe *
Rituals, Akademie der Kunste, Berlin *
Phantom of Desire, Neue Galerie, Graz *
Absolut Generations, Palazzo Zenobio, 50th Venice Biennale *
The Anxious Creation, Galeria d'Arte Moderna e Contemporanea, Verona *
a body / a cialo (with John Coplans), Center of Contemporary Art, Gdansk
Dog in Polish Art, Galeria Arsenal, Bialystok

2004
Prym, BWA, Zielona Gora / Foksal Gallery Foundation, Warsaw *
The skull and other still lives, Atelier 19, Academy of Fine Arts, Poznan
Joyce in Art, Royal Hibernian Academy, Dublin *
Art Poznan, Stary Browar, Poznan *
Rohkunstbau, Wasserschoss Gross Leuthen, Spreewald *
N(e)orretratos, Galeria Juana de Aizpuru, Madrid
Out of place, Galerie Nordenhake, Berlin
Transcultures, National Museum of Contemporary Art, Athens *

Eclipse, White Cube, London *
Continental Breakfast, The Public Bath, Belgrad *
mysla, slowem, forma, obrazem, Stary Browar, Poznan *
Niose przed soba lustro, Galeria Szara, Cieszyn *
Amongst differences, Galeria Hansgrohe-Aquademia, Tarnow Podgorny *
Warsaw – Moskwa / Moskwa – Warsaw, Galeria Zacheta, Warsaw *
Sygnowano Stanko, Fabryka Trzciny, Warsaw

2005
non ho capito le ultime parole (with Alfredo Pirri), Instituto Polacco and Volume, Rome *
Czas kultury, Arsenal, Poznan *
Horyzont zderzen, Stara Rzeznia, Poznan *
Freiheit und Verantwortung, Universitat der Kunste, Berlin
Idyl, Middelheimmuseum, Antwerp *
Experience of Art, 51st Venice Biennale *
Positioning / In the New Reality of Europe, National Museum of Art, Osaka / Hiroshima City Museum of Contemporary Art / Museum of Contemporary Art, Tokyo *
Chocolate Grinder No.3 / Continental Breakfast, Comitato Trieste Contemporanea, Trieste *

2006
Sublime Embrace, Art Gallery of Hamilton *
Zones of Contact, 15th Biennale of Sydney *
Y Ahora Sin Ti ..., Galeria Juana de Aizpuru, Madrid
Ideal City / Invisible Cities, Zamosc and Potsdam *
Still Points of the Turning World, SITE Santa Fe Biennial *
Hot/Cold: summer loving, Galeria Zacheta, Warsaw *
Polemos: the work of art: conflict and resolution, Fortress of Gavi near Alessandria *
Terytoria, Centrum Kultury, Lublin *
The Form Is Emptiness – The Emptiness Is Form, Fabryka Schindlera, Krakow / Sektor I, GCK Katowice *
The Exotic Journey Ends, Fundacja Galerii Foksal, Warsaw *
The 80s: A Topology, Museu Serralves, Porto *

2007
Beyond (with Alfredo Pirri), Bunkier Sztuki, Krakow *
Medium. Post. Mortem, Centre Wallon d'Art Contemporain, la Chataigneraie / Muzeum Narodowe, Szczecin
Archicooking, Wroclaw
New Agora / Internacional Academy of Intercultural Dialog, The Synagogue's Square, Wroclaw *
Ulica Prozna, Warsaw
no title (with Rafal Jakubowicz, Marzena Nowak), Dvir Gallery, Tel Aviv
Pan Topor dzis nie przyjdzie, Rondo Sztuki, Katowice

2008

Still / Motion, Prefectural Art Museum, Mie, Japan / National Museum of Art, Osaka / Tokyo Metropolitan Museum of Photography, Tokyo *
8784h, Galeria X-ray, Lubon
Bifurkacje, Centum Rzezby Polskiej, Oronsko
Minimum maksimum, BWA, Lublin
Souvenirs, University of Ben Gurion, Beersheba
Re-Reading the Future, International Triennale, National Gallery, Prague
deca-dance, Museu Nacional do Conjunto Cultural da Republica, Brasilia
Involved, ShanghART H - Space, Shanghai *
Sztuka cenniejsza niz zloto, Muzeum Sztuki Nowoczesnej, Warsaw

2009

Horizontabschreitung (with Ursula Schulz-Dornburg), Kunstparterre, Munich *
I could live in Africa, Ursula Blickle Stiftung, Kraichtal-Unterowisheim
On the Spot, Ein Hod
Lichtzwang, Dvir Gallery, Tel Aviv
Sound Invasion, Galeria Zacheta, Warsaw *
A Pair of Left Shoes, Bochum Museum
artboom, Plac Niepodleglosci, Krakow
Urban Legend, Poznan *
Compas in Hand, Museum of Modern Art, New York *
This is Sculpture, Tate Liverpool

Solo exhibition catalogues

Percepta Patris Mei Servivi Semper. Galeria Pokaz, Warsaw 1986; text by Anda Rottenberg.

River. Galeria Labirynt 2, Lublin 1989; text by Maria Morzuch.

Good God. Galeria Dziekanka, Warsaw 1990; text by Joanna Kiliszek.

xxx. De Appel Foundation, Amsterdam 1991; text by Christoph Blasé.

April / My body cannot do everything I ask for. Galeria Foksal, Warsaw 1991; text by Andrzej Przywara.

bitte. Museum Haus Lange, Krefeld 1992; text by Julian Heynen.

36,6. The Renaissance Society, Chicago and MIT List Visual Arts Center, Cambridge MA 1992; texts by Julian Heynen and Peter Schjeldahl.

37,I (cont.). Padiglione della Polonia, XLV Biennale di Venezia, Venice 1993; text by Anda Rottenberg.

Die Rampe. Van Abbemuseum, Eindhoven and Museum Sztuki, Lodz 1994; texts by Jan Debbaut, Maria Morzuch, Selma Klein Essink, Anda Rottenberg and an interview with the artist by Jaromir Jedlinski.

Winterhilfsverein. Moderna Galerija, Ljubljana 1994; text by Zdenka Badovinac.

Dawn. Tate Gallery, London 1995; text by Frances Morris.

Selection. Museet for Samtidskunst, Oslo 1997; texts by Karin Hellandsjo, Andrzej Przywara, Neal Benezra and interview with the artist by Adam Szymczyk.

a,e,i,o,u. Galeria Foksal, Warsaw 1997; text by Adam Szymczyk.

Revision 1986–1997. IVAM, Valencia 1997; texts by SJ Beyzym, Juan Vicente Aliaga and interview with the artist by Juan Vicente Aliaga.

Miroslaw Balka: A Memorial. Statens konstråd, Stockholm 1998; texts by Ann-Sofie Noring and Annika Ohrner.

Hygiene. Galeria Labirynt 2, Lublin 1998; text by Marek Gozdziewski.

sza. Galeria Foksal, Warsaw 1999.

Between meals. National Museum of Art, Osaka 2000; texts by Akiko Kasuya and Miroslaw Balka.

Around 21˚15'00"E 52˚06'17"N +GO–GO (1985–2001). Galeria Zacheta, Warsaw and SMAK, Gent 2001; texts by Bart de Bare, Magdelena Kardasz, Anda Rottenberg and Rafal Jakubowicz.

Ruhe. BWA, Zielona Góra, 2001; text by Rafal Jakubowicz.

eclipse. Kröller-Müller Museum, Otterlo 2001; text by Andree van der Kerckhove.

cekaonica. Museum of Contemporary Art, Zagreb 2002; text by Nada Beros.

dig,dug,dug. Douglas Hyde Gallery, Dublin 2002; text by John Hutchinson.

winterreise. Galeria Starmach, Krakow 2003; texts by Mieczyslaw Porebski and interview with artist by Rafal Jakubowicz.

Bon voyage. Musées de la Ville de Strasbourg 2004; ed. Emmanuel Guigon; texts by Emmanuel Guigon, Juan Vicente Aliaga and Stephane Lentz.

hipnoza. Galeria Arsenal, Bialystok 2005; text by Marek Wasilewski.

Lichtzwang. K21, Dusseldorf 2006; text by Julian Heynen.

AAA + rauchsignale. Museum of Modern and Contemporary Art, Rijeka 2007; text by Leila Topic.

Reflejos condicionados. Fundación Marcelino Botín, Santander 2007; conversation between Juan Vicente Aliaga, Julian Heynen and Miroslaw Balka and text by Juan Vicente Aliaga.

Tristes Tropiques. Irish Museum of Modern Art, Dublin 2007; texts by Claude Lévi-Strauss, Enrique Juncosa and Caoimhim Mac Giolla Leith.

Jetzt. WRO Art Center, Wroclaw 2008; text by Piotr Krajewski.

17 x 23,5 x 1,6. White Cube, London 2008 to coincide with *Nothere*; texts by Michael Archer and Zygmunt Bauman.

Gravity. University of Massachusetts, Amherst 2009; text by Barbara London; interview with the artist by Gregory Salzman.

Photographic and Collection Credits

p.15, © Tuca Vieira
p.16, Getty Images/ Zack Seckler
p.19, (left) Ignacy Balka
p.19, (right) Getty Images/ Gary Cralle
p.22, Dean Terry
p.24, (top) © Pierre Vauthey/ Corbis Sygma
p.24, (bottom)/25 (top) Tate Photography.
Collection Tate
p.25, (bottom) Mary Evans Picture Library
p.27, Photograph © Piotr Tomczyk. Collection
Muzeum Sztuki, Lodz
p.28, Collection courtesy the artist and Galerie
Nordenhake, Stockholm. Edition 2 of 2
p.30, (top) Martyna Balka. Collection the artist
p.30, (bottom) Courtesy the artist
and White Cube, London
p.31, Johannes Hähle. Collection Archives of the
Hamburg Institute for Social Research
p.33, (right) Tate Photography. Collection Tate
p.34, (left and right) Volker Döhn (left) Private
Collection (right) Private Collection
p.36, (left) © 2008. Photo Scala, Florence.
Collection Russian State Museum, St Petersburg
p.36, (right) Wellcome Library, London
p.37, Photograph Miroslaw Balka. Courtesy the
artist and White Cube, London
p.38, Photograph Martyna Balka. Private Collection
p.41, © Dundee Contemporary Arts. Photograph by
Ruth Clark. Collection Israel Museum, Jerusalem
p.42, Photograph Miroslaw Balka. Courtesy the artist
and Galerie Nordenhake, Stockholm
p.43, Photograph Piotr Ligier. Collection of the artist
p.45, Courtesy the artist and White Cube, London
p.47, Courtesy the artist
p.48, The Bridgeman Art Library/Private Collection/
The Stapleton Collection
p.49, © The Trustees of the British Museum
p.51, Bibliothèque nationale de France
p.52, Photograph Martyna Balka. Collection of the artist
p.56, (left) Collection Marcantonio Vilaça, Brasília
p.56, (right) © Jerzy Gladykowski, courtesy the
Foksal Gallery, Warsaw. Collection the artist
p.64, Robson Bolsoni. Collection Museo Bispo
do Rosario, Rio de Janeiro. Produced by Open
Art Projects
p.65, Collection Diocesan Museum, Siedlce
p.67, SSPL. Collection Science Museum, London
p.70, Photograph Galleria Raffaella Cortese.
Courtesy Private Collection, Italy
p.73, Horace Bristol/Corbis

p.75, © RMN (Collection Musée d'Orsay).
p.76, Tate Photography. Collection Tate
p.77, Courtesy 'The World of Lygia Clark' Cultural
Association
p.78, © 2003. Photo Scala Florence/ HIP
p.81, General Research & Reference Division,
Schomburg Centre for Research in Black Culture,
The New York Public Library, Astor, Lenox and Tilden
Foundations
p.83, Photograph Miroslaw Balka, courtesy the artist
p.85, Private collection, courtesy Gladstone Gallery,
New York
p.86, Photograph Todd White Art Photography.
Private collection, courtesy White Cube, London
p.88, Courtesy the artist and White Cube, London
p.91, Catholic Resources: Reverend Felix Just
(www.catholic-resources.org)
p.92, © Mohamed Messara/epa/Corbis
p.94, Photograph © Jerzy Gladykowski, courtesy
the Foksal Gallery. Collection of the artist
p.96, Photograph Jan Gaworski, Foundation Egit.
Deposited at the Centre of Polish Sculpture, Oronsko
p.98, © John Haynes
p.104, (top) © Jerome Minet/Kipa/Corbis
p.104, (bottom) Tate Photography. Collection Tate
p.105, (top) Courtesy the artist and Barbara
Gladstone Gallery
p.106, Tate Photography. Collection Tate
p.107, Photograph Miroslaw Balka. Courtesy the artist
p.109, BFI Stills
p.112, Photographs Miroslaw Balka
p.113, Wellcome Library, London
p.117, Photograph National Museum of Art, Osaka
p.118, (top) Collection Roger Thorp
p.118, (bottom) Collection Roger Thorp
p.119, (top) Getty Images/ Bruno Vincent
p.119, (bottom) © NTPL/ Andreas von Einsiedel
p.120, (top left) © Keystone. Courtesy the Natural
History Museum, London
p.120, (top right) Collection Roger Thorp
p.120, (bottom) Collection Roger Thorp
p.121, © 1990. Photo Scala, Florence. Collection
Pomorskie Museum, Gdansk
p.130–44 Sam Irons

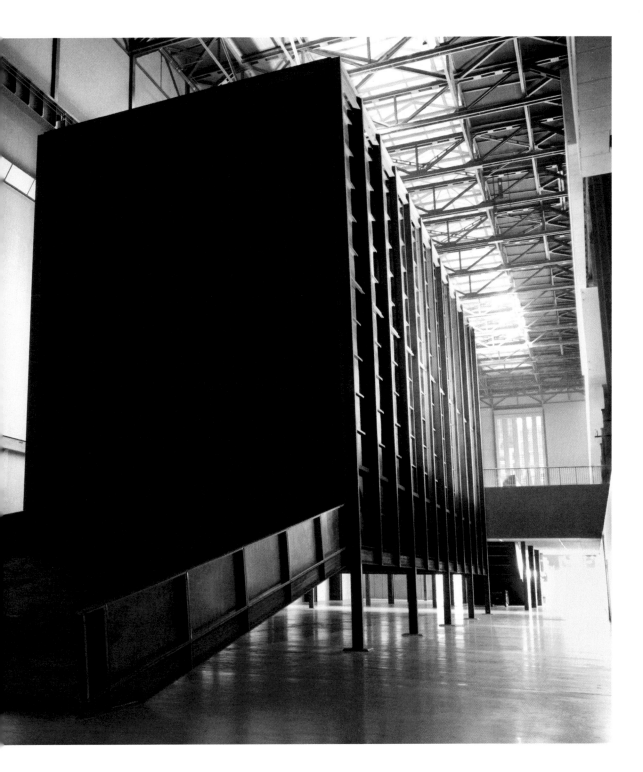